# The Wolf Shall Dwell with the Lamb

Aaron,

Thank your for your commitment to dismantling racism in the Diocese of Western Michigan as we strive to "...respect the dignity of every human being."

May God bless your efforts for the sake of the Kingdom.

+ Robert

Also by Eric H. F. Law
published by Chalice Press

*The Bush was Blazing but not Consumed*

*Inclusion*

*Sacred Acts, Holy Change*

# The Wolf Shall Dwell with the Lamb

## A Spirituality for Leadership in a Multicultural Community

by
**Eric H. F. Law**

CHALICE
PRESS

ST. LOUIS, MISSOURI

Scripture quotations not otherwise designated are from the *New Revised Standard Version Bible*, copyright 1989, Division of Christian Education of the National Council of Churches of Christ in the United States of America and are used by permission.

Scripture quotations marked RSV are from the *Revised Standard Version* of the Bible, copyrighted 1946, 1952, © 1971, 1973.

Cover illustration: Chris Vculek
Art Director: Michael Domínguez

10                                                           03  04

Visit Chalice Press on the World Wide Web at
www.chalicepress.com

**Library of Congress Cataloging–in–Publication Data**

Law, Eric H. F.
   The wolf shall dwell with the lamb / by Eric H.F. Law.
   ISBN 0-8272-4231-X
   1. Christianity and culture.   2. Peace—Religious aspects—Christianity.   3. Power—Religious aspects—Christianity.
   4. Intercultural communication.   5. Intercultural education.
   I. Title
   BR115.C8L378   1993       261.8'73       93–9205

Printed in the United States of America

## Dedication:

*To my parents,*
*Law Kwok-Nam and Tam Un-Oi,*
*who had the courage*
*to leave behind*
*everything they knew*
*and immigrated*
*to the United States*
*and provided me with my first*
*major intercultural experience*

# Contents

# Introduction

I was invited to be the music minister for a national Episcopal Church conference. In preparing for it, I compiled a list of songs that I believed to be "inclusive." On the opening night of the conference, I led the gathering in singing hymns with different cultural origins. To close the evening celebration, I thought it would be appropriate to sing "Lift Every Voice and Sing," sometimes referred to as the "African-American national anthem."

I had heard this song being sung by an African-American congregation and I appreciated the energy and spirit they brought to it. Outside of such a context, the energy is often missing. With the help of the accompanist, I encouraged the gathering to sing "Lift Every Voice and Sing" with more vigor and spirit, and invited them to watch my signal to hold and emphasize certain notes. I was hoping that this effort would make our singing of the hymn more "authentic." In the middle of the song, I picked up a tambourine and added what I believed to be appropriate accents. At the end, some people applauded.

While I was enjoying the praises coming my way, an African-American woman approached.

"I don't know how much you know about this song," she said to me. "Since you're Asian, I don't expect you to know that. So I'm sure you didn't mean it, but I have to say this: I am deeply offended by the way you did that song."

I was not prepared to hear such a statement. I thought I was being very inclusive and authentic. I swallowed my pride and said, "I'm sorry. Can you tell me what I did wrong so that I won't do it again?"

"This song came out of the struggle of African Americans. It should be sung with more dignity," she replied.

The only response I could muster was, "Thank you for sharing that with me." I thought to myself: what a trite answer. Did I really mean it? Or did I just want to get rid of her?

I did not sleep much that night. I kept replaying the scene over and over again, unwilling to face up to what I had done. From past experience, I knew that whenever I went around in circles, I was surely avoiding something—usually pain. In the middle of the night, I finally admitted that I was hurt. I was hurt because I thought I was trying to be inclusive. In fact, I thought I was doing a good job at it. The part that hurt the most was that not only was my effort to be inclusive not recognized but it actually had the opposite effect.

The next morning, I addressed the gathering. "Before we begin this morning, I would like to explain the principles behind the choice of hymns in this conference. I tried to be inclusive in picking hymns with various ethnic and cultural origins. Also, in singing and teaching these songs, I attempted to sing them as authentically as possible. However, sometimes I may make mistakes in my effort to do that. It's like when someone invited me to dinner and in their effort to include me, they attempted to cook what they believed to be an authentic Chinese meal. It consisted of chop suey and egg fu yung." They laughed. "Well, sometimes, I do that too. This is part of the pain of living in a multicultural community. If I commit myself to be inclusive, I must face the danger of making such mistakes. So, I want to make a deal with you. If at any time during this conference, I abuse a song from a culture with which you are more familiar, I expect you to let me know so that I can continue to learn and grow from my mistakes. In this process, I also invite to you to recognize my intention to be inclusive." Graciously, they agreed.

I felt the same kind of danger while I was writing this book. I kept saying, "What if I am wrong? What if I offend people in writing this book? What if...?" Then I realized that I am not perfect, and that I probably will inspire some people and offend others. I will just have to face the consequences of presenting this material in written form.

What I have attempted to do in this book is to begin the dialogue and theological reflection on what it means, spiritually and practically, to be a leader in a multicultural community. I have approached this topic through biblical reflection, an analysis of the differences in the perception of power in different cultures, theological reflection, and case studies. In the appendixes, I present some practical processes and ideas that I have tested in my work as a consultant in multicultural ministry. I would invite you, the reader, to try them out in your work and ministry. Your feedback is most welcome so that we all can continue to learn to be better leaders in a multicultural world.

I want to thank the Los Angeles chapter of the National Conference of Christians and Jews (NCCJ) for getting me started in doing interreligious and intercultural dialogue, especially Lucky Altman. I want to thank my friend Mark Gardner for reading the first draft of this book and giving me constructive feedback. I also thank David Polk for his enthusiasm and support of this book. I thank Steve Rutberg for his patience while I was working night and day on this project. Finally, I want to thank all the groups I have worked within the last three years. Their willingness to experiment with me and give me feedback is what has made this book a reality.

## How to Reach the Author

Eric H. F. Law can be contacted by sending an E-mail to chalice@cbp21.com, which will be forwarded.

# CHAPTER 1

# The "Peaceable Realm" as a Vision of an Ideal Multicultural Community

The wolf shall dwell with the lamb,
 and the leopard shall lie down with the kid,
and the calf and the lion and the fatling together,
 and a little child shall lead them.
The cow and the bear shall feed;
 their young shall lie down together;
 and the lion shall eat straw like the ox.
The sucking child shall play over the hole of the asp,
 and the weaned child shall put his hand on the
 adder's den.
They shall not hurt or destroy in all my holy mountain;
for the earth shall be full of the knowledge of the LORD
 as the waters cover the sea.
Isaiah 11:6–9, RSV

Ten years ago, I spent a semester in France studying the audiovisual communication of faith. For the first time I participated in a multicultural gathering in which three languages were used. The experienced instructors divided the participants into two major groups according to the languages that we spoke—an English group and a French/Spanish group. The two groups lived in separate housing

1

facilities. We received instruction separately most of the time except for major lectures that were translated simultaneously. At the beginning of the program, we did many things together—field trips, discussions, planning, worship, and eating. The English group, of which I was a part, tended to enjoy these gatherings because most of the time we were doing activities that we liked.

As time went by, the two groups had fewer and fewer opportunities to gather except during lunch time and occasional large community celebrations. Finally, the English group questioned the instructors concerning the lack of opportunities to mingle with the French/Spanish group. The response was: "We decided not to put the two groups together anymore. We have had too many complaints from the French and Spanish group. They said that whenever the two groups were together, the English group always took control and the needs of the French/Spanish-speaking group were always ignored." Upon hearing this, the English group, myself included, was taken totally by surprise. I had no idea that we were dominating and certainly was not conscious of the other group's feeling. Some of us felt bad about it while others denied that they were dominating. Some tried to convince the French/Spanish group that they should not feel excluded.

This incident was a typical example of how cultural differences set up a frustrating power dynamic in a multicultural situation. Through my years of traveling and working with groups, I have asked people of all colors to share their multicultural group experiences with me. Eighty percent of them described the same frustration. Whenever two or three culturally diverse groups come together, the white English-speaking group most likely sets the agenda, does most of the talking and decision making, and, in some cases, feels guilty that the other ethnic groups do not participate in the decision making.

I observed the same scenario over and over again. For a long time, I felt totally powerless about changing the course of these encounters. I call it the "wolf and lamb" scenario. When a wolf is together with other wolves, everything is fine.

When a lamb is together with other lambs, everything is safe and sound. But if you put a wolf and a lamb together, inevitably something bad is going to happen. Some people are so disheartened by it that they are giving up the idea of integration altogether. Many white English-speaking people enter a multicultural situation with dread and apprehension that the other might accuse them of domination and oppression. Many people of color stop accepting invitations to multicultural gatherings, knowing that they will be ignored and put down one more time and that the result will be a waste of their time.

If we stretch the analogy of the "wolf and lamb" scenario further, one might say that the cultures of the world are as numerous as the kinds of animals inhabiting this earth. Each culture has its own characteristics, values, and customs. Some are perceived as strong and some as weak. Some are more aggressive and some are considered passive and timid. People in one culture survive as individuals while people in another culture find their own liveliness as part of larger groupings. If cultures are analogous to the different animals, then Isaiah 11:6–9 becomes a vision of culturally diverse peoples living together in harmony and peace. This passage is known popularly as the "Peaceable Kingdom." I prefer to call it the "Peaceable Realm." For me, the word *Kingdom* has too many connotations of the hierarchical human system that the passage challenges. *Realm* may be a more neutral term. It connotes a state of being. It can also imply a philosophical essence, as in "realm" of thoughts.

In order for the animals to co-exist in this Peaceable Realm, very "unnatural" behaviors are required from all who are involved. How can a wolf, a leopard, or a lion not attack a lamb, a calf, or a child for food? At least our fairy tales taught us to believe that. How can a lamb or a calf not run when it sees a lion or a leopard coming close? How can a lion eat straw like an ox when a lion is known to be a meat eater? It goes against an animal's "instinct" to be in this vision of the Peaceable Realm. Perhaps that is what is required of human beings if we are to live together peacefully with each other. Perhaps we have to go against the "instinct" of our cultures in order for us to stop replaying the fierce-devouring-the-small scenario of intercultural encounter. Perhaps, when all of us have learned how to do that, we may be able to regain our innocence like a child playing over the hole of the asp and putting her hand on the adder's den and not being afraid anymore.

When I use the word *culture* in this context, I refer to ethnic culture—the values, beliefs, arts, food, customs, clothing, family and social organizations, and government of a given people in a given period. It is a known fact that ethnic cultures differ from each other to varying degrees. If all cultures were the same, I would not be writing this book. How do cultural differences come about? Here is a hypothesis that I discovered in a very useful book called *Developing Intercultural Awareness*. Before there were planes, boats, trains, television, movies and magazines, people lived in various parts of the world in isolated communities. Because of differences in climate and natural resources, people developed different ways to meet the basic necessities of life such as food, shelter, community, family, etc. These solutions to life's basic necessities evolved into different cultures. These cultures are neither good nor bad. They are just different. However, because these cultures were developed in isolation, a person brought up in one particular culture, having never seen or experienced a different culture, believes that his or her culture's way of doing things is the right way. This is called ethnocentricity. There is no problem when a person who was raised in one culture stays within that cultural group because everyone in the group knows, understands, and shares the same worldview. Problems arise when a person from one culture is put into another culture. Conflict becomes inevitable.[1]

It is helpful to look at culture in two parts: external and internal. External culture is the conscious part of culture. It is the part that we can see, taste, and hear. It consists of

---

[1] L. Robert Kohls, *Developing Intercultural Awareness* (Washington, DC: The Society for Intercultural Education, Training and Research, 1981), p.65.

acknowledged beliefs and values. It is explicitly learned and can be easily changed. However, this constitutes only a small part of our culture. The major part is the internal part, which consists of the unconscious beliefs, thought patterns, values, and myths that affect everything we do and see. It is implicitly learned and is very hard to change. A good image that can help us understand this better is an iceberg.[2] An iceberg has a small visible part above water and a very large and irregular part under the water. The part above water can represent external culture and the part under the surface can represent internal culture. What I mean by the "instinct" of our culture is this internal part that is not conscious and is very hard to change. Let's examine the two parts of culture in more detail.

Most of the time, when we use the word *culture*, we mean the kinds of things that we see and hear—music, dance, food and art, etc. These are only the external cultural traits that are articulated and therefore observable. They are explicitly learned behaviors, knowledge, and beliefs. One is conscious of these external cultural traits and, therefore, they are easily changed. For example, I grew up in a Chinese household in which we ate only with chopsticks. Using chopsticks is definitely a learned behavior. Chinese were not born with chopsticks in their hands. Neither were Europeans born with a knife and fork in their hands. The objective of using chopsticks is very simple: to get food into your mouth so you won't be hungry. The first time I went to a British restaurant, it was very puzzling to see the layout of forks, knives, spoons, glasses, and stacks of plates and bowls. My ethnocentric self thought: this is quite ridiculous when a pair of chopsticks and a rice bowl would be much easier, better, and faster. After my initial prejudiced reaction, I realized that the objective here was the same: to get

---

[2]The image of the iceberg has been used in organization development training for a long time. The first time I encountered this analogy being used in intercultural analysis was in Gary R. Weaver's "Understanding and Coping with Cross-Cultural Adjustment Stress" in *Cross-Cultural Orientation: New Conceptualization and Application*, ed. by R. Michael Paige (University Press of America, 1986), pp.134–146.

food into your mouth. So with some practice, I learned very quickly the proper way to eat with knives and forks.

Let me offer another example. When I was a teenager in Hong Kong, I acquired a taste for American folk music. I liked it because it was simple music and easy to learn. I used to sing "This Land Is Your Land" in Hong Kong and had no idea what it all meant. When I immigrated to the United States in 1971, suddenly the music of Bob Dylan, Woody Guthrie, and Peter, Paul and Mary had a context. Within this context I consciously embraced many of the values of that era and began to write the same kind of music myself. As I evolved with the '70s and '80s, my philosophy, beliefs, and values changed and I did not stubbornly hold on to the ideals of the '60s. Because I consciously adopted these values and beliefs, I usually could change them with ease after some reflection, research, or rationalization. I believe this flexibility came from my consciousness of embracing those values. I deliberately take up an idea and I can easily leave it behind. I would have had a more difficult struggle had I been born and raised in the '60s in the United States, because many of these values and beliefs would be unconscious to me and, therefore, very hard to change.

However, external culture constitutes only a small part of our cultural iceberg. The larger part is the hidden internal culture that governs the way we think, perceive, and behave unconsciously. This is what I call the "instinct" of our cultures. *Instinct* as defined in Webster's Dictionary is an "inborn tendency to behave in a way characteristic of a species: natural, unacquired response to stimuli...." The cultural environment in which we grew up shapes the way we behave and think. Implicit in this cultural environment are the cultural myths, values, beliefs, and thought patterns that influence our behavior and the way we perceive and respond to our surroundings. Most of the time, we are unconscious of their existence. They are implicitly learned and are very difficult to change. We are conditioned to react to our environment in particular ways that are not very different from an instinctual physical reaction to stimuli. When we feel the sting of a needle, we withdraw. In the same way, we interpret what we see according to these unconscious values and thought patterns and we respond in an instinctual way according to these beliefs and values regarding what is proper and right.

Internal culture is like the air we breathe. We need it to survive and make sense of the world that we live in, but we may not be conscious of it. If you put an object with both red and green designs in front of a red background, you will see only the green design. The red designs will blend into the background and become less noticeable. However, if you put the same object in front of a green background, you will see the red design much better and not notice the green design. Internal cultures are like these backgrounds. They influence the way we perceive our relationships and environment, often unconsciously. Internal cultural differences, then, are like the difference between the red and the green backgrounds. It is not a matter of different ways of eating or different clothing or languages. It is more a matter of perceptions and feelings. The same event may be perceived very differently by two culturally different persons because the two different internal cultures highlight different parts of the same incident. This internal, unconscious part of culture constitutes a much larger part of our culture. To discover the unconscious, implicit part of our culture is a lifelong process. Some of us go through life like a fish in the stream and never know that we are living in water.

As a Chinese American with a somewhat complicated cultural makeup, I still surprise myself when I discover a new aspect of my internal culture. For example, one of my "instinctual" reactions to conflict is to be silent. It took me a long time to recognize this internal cultural trait. Every internal cultural trait has a value behind it. To be culturally sensitive is to recognize these values in ourselves and in others. After much reflection and help from friends and spiritual directors, I discovered that, growing up as the youngest child in a Chinese family, I used silence as a way to protect myself. Silence in my family is a form of protest. It still works for me today but only in the context of my family. I was eating dinner and conversing freely with my parents one evening last year. In the middle of the interchange, my father said, "Eric, I think you should go to medical school and become a doctor. Look at Mr. Wong's son. He was a little guy then, but he made it. He is a doctor now. If he can do it, you can too."

I had not heard my father mention medical school since I was ordained, so I was quite disturbed by what he was saying at this stage of my life. My ego was bruised. Here I was, thirty-four years old, an ordained Episcopal priest, with two degrees. I traveled all over the country to teach, consult, and give workshops. I composed music and had put out three recordings. And my father wanted me to be a doctor! While I was steaming over what he said, I grew silent. I could get mad and confront him. I could stand up and walk away, but I simply stopped talking. My mother immediately sensed my protest. She, in her gentle way, said, "Your father thinks you are still a little boy sometimes." Then to my father she said, "I don't think being a doctor is so great anymore. In this country, you can go broke paying the malpractice insurance. In Hong Kong, it's a different story. At least you get respect. Here you don't even get respect. At the blink of an eye, you get sued." That took care of it. My father never talked about medical school again. I at that moment resumed my conversation with my parents on another topic. My silence was interpreted correctly as a protest against my father's lack of sensitivity.

However, I was not conscious of this implicit cultural trait for a long time. In a white English-speaking environment, when I disagreed with what was going on, all I knew was that people ignored me. I could not understand why they did not read my message of disapproval. I did not realize that they probably interpreted my silence as consent, indifference, or incompetence. Even though I am conscious of this now, my initial reaction to most conflict is still silence. This has been an implicit value for me for a long time, and it is very hard to change. However, I have learned to recognize this internal cultural trait and to take positive steps to determine the appropriateness of this behavior. For example, if I am in a first-generation Chinese environment, silence is still an appropriate behavior to communicate dissent. But if I am in a white English-speaking situation, I must recognize that silence will be misinterpreted and I must find ways to verbalize my disagreement.

Cultural clashes do not happen on the external, conscious cultural level. We can easily change behaviors based on conscious values and beliefs in order to adapt and accommodate to the situation. We can even modify our acknowledged beliefs and values with some intellectual reasoning and reflection. Most cultural clashes happen on the internal unconscious level—on the instinctual level where the parties involved are not even conscious of why they feel and react the way they do. Since each person thinks only in her own thought pattern, she cannot even understand why the others do not perceive things the way she does. It is like two icebergs hitting each other under the water. On the surface they appear to be at a safe distance from each other. This communication breakdown creates a mutual animosity, causing a need to protect oneself. This defense usually comes in the form of putting down the other or assuming one's own culture is superior.[3]

To be interculturally sensitive, we need to examine the internal instinctual part of our own culture. This means revealing unconscious values and thought patterns so that we will not simply react from our cultural instinct. The more we learn about our internal culture, the more we are aware of how our cultural values and thought patterns differ from others. Knowing this difference will help us make self-adjustments in order to live peacefully with people from other cultures. A lion needs to know that its predatory instinct can hurt the calf and therefore must temper it. A lion might even

---

[3]The stage of "Defense" in Cross-Cultural Orientation can be found in the research of Milton J. Bennett, "A Developmental Approach to Training for Intercultural Sensitivity," in *Theories and Methods in Cross-Cultural Orientation*, ed. by Judith N. Martin, *International Journal of Intercultural Relations*, Vol. 5, No. 2 (New York/Oxford/Beijing/Frankfurt/Sao Paulo/Sydney/Tokyo/Toronto: Pergamon Press, 1986), pp.179–196; and Milton J. Bennett, "Towards Ethnorelativism: A Developmental Model of Intercultural Sensitivity," in *Cross-Cultural Orientation*, pp.27–69.

become a vegetarian for a while in order to live in the Peaceable Realm. A lamb needs to know that when it sees a wolf, its instinct is to run. It needs to learn to be strong and stand firm to face the wolf as an equal in the Peaceable Realm. If we are conscious of the instinctual part of our cultures, we can better adjust our behavior and attitudes so that we can realize the vision of the Peaceable Realm in this diverse multicultural society.

This is not going to be easy. Uncovering our own internal culture will take a lifetime. We can speed up the process by seeking to encounter others who are different. In the encounter, others can help us see ourselves from a different cultural point of view. It is like a fish being pulled out of the water and discovering for the first time that the water had been its total life context. A fish out of the water is not comfortable. Its life is in danger. That is how it feels sometimes when we are being pulled outside our cultural water so that we can see what our culture looks like from the other's point of view. We can feel very threatened and insecure. Our instinct is to jump back into our cultural water. Our instinct is to run and hide. But as Christians, we are often called to go against our instinct. Jesus Christ invites us to take up the cross and follow him. Who would want to take up the cross—an instrument of the cruelest capital punishment? It goes against our instinct of survival to embrace pain, suffering, and death. Yet, Jesus invites us to face them squarely and not be afraid. The good news is that Jesus has done it. He has shown us that there is resurrection and new life. Our initiation through baptism is a symbol of our dying to the old self and participating in the new life through Jesus Christ. Therefore, I invite the reader to take courage, to go against our instinct, to uncover our own cultural waters, and to live in the uncharted intercultural waters of the Peaceable Realm.

I pray for a world one day
Where no one needs to be afraid
A world that's full of the knowledge of peace
As the waters cover the sea
As the waters cover the sea

Fill me with your love, O God
Pour your justice over me
Flood me with your power to forgive
And soak me in your peace
As the waters cover the sea.

# CHAPTER 2

# What Makes a Lamb Different from a Wolf? Understanding Cultural Differences in the Perception of Power

> "What does the LORD require of you but to do justice, and to love kindness, and to walk humbly with your God?"
>
> Micah 6:8

As a Christian, doing justice is part of my calling and duty. Justice means equal distribution of power and privilege among all people. In the vision of the Peaceable Realm, the balanced distribution of power among the animals is essential. However, most of the time, we think of peace as the lack of conflict and the assurance of protection. Therefore, in the name of peace, many social systems exercise authority to control people's behavior. The rationale is that if people are fearful of the punishment prescribed by the law of the system, they are less likely to hurt others or destroy properties. Fear is the operating principle in this kind of system. It is like the lion, the king of the forest, saying, "We will have peace by doing what I tell you; if you don't, I will devour you."

Our vision of the Peaceable Realm is not based on fear. Instead, it is based on the lack of fear. "The sucking child shall play over the hole of the asp, and the weaned child shall put his hand on the adder's den" (Isaiah 11:8, RSV). This lack of fear is created by the even distribution of power. The lamb is equal to the wolf. The calf is equal to the lion. Therefore, they can live peacefully together. True peace cannot be attained without justice. To do justice, then, is to be able to see and recognize the uneven distribution of power and to take steps to change the system so that we can redistribute power equally.

Can the church be God's holy mountain on which people from diverse cultures "shall not hurt or destroy" each other? The church, in the most basic way, is the bringing together of people, sometimes from very diverse cultural backgrounds. When people from diverse cultures come together, the power dynamic in which one group dominates and claims more power than another is inevitable. In a multicultural community, doing the work of justice requires us to understand the different perceptions of power from different cultural points of view. If we can understand the internal cultural values behind why some people seem to be powerless and others powerful, then we can understand the root cause of this "wolf and lamb" scenario. With this knowledge, we can then work toward finding new ways of being where power is more evenly distributed.

In this chapter, we will dig deeply into our internal cultures, looking specifically at the differences in perceptions of personal power among the different cultures. The perception of personal power is our own understanding of our ability to change our environment. In terms of interpersonal relationships, the perception of power is our sense of authority and ability to influence and control others. More often than not, this perception of power is unconscious. It is part of the "instinctual" culture that I mentioned in the previous chapter. Here is another way of looking at this: The perception of power is one's degree of acceptance of inequality. If I accept an inequality of power and authority as a given, then I will not see myself as having the need or the power to change it. If I do not accept inequality as a given, and believe instead that everyone should be equal to me, then I must see myself as having the power to change my environment and the system in order to attain that equality.

The perception of power is different from the reality of having that power. Middle-class white Americans are taught to believe that they have the power to change society and to make a difference. In reality, the upper class is the group that really has this power and privilege. In fact, in recent years the economic and political power of the middle class has diminished. However, both the middle and upper classes have the same perception of their personal power. This perception of power expresses itself through one's behavior and attitude, and very often it is unconscious. If a white middle-class person is mistreated by the system her first reaction would be to speak up, fight back, and undo this injustice. This is the behavior of a person who perceived herself to have power. A person who perceived himself to be powerless would just accept the injustice as a part of life that a powerless person endures. Many middle-class white Americans, who realized that their economic and political power was diminishing, tried to be in "solidarity with" the poor but found their efforts fruitless and frustrating. This is because even though in reality they may be equals in terms of economic and political power, their attitude and behavior based on their difference in perceptions of power still separate them.

Once I gave a presentation on racism at a conference. Afterward, a young man confronted me in the hallway. He said, "How could you talk about white people as if they are all the same? We are not all racists. We are not all oppressors. I found it very disturbing to hear you stereotype us while you are talking about undoing racism." I tried to explain without being too defensive, knowing that something else was at work here. I had noticed how, all through the conference, he would speak out on how whites were oppressed too and did not deserve to be stereotyped. But the responses from the people of color were: "Now you know how we feel; the few moments that you felt the sting of discrimination is how we felt all our lives." These responses were by no means friendly. I watched this man withdraw more and more as the day wore on. As I explained how I decided to speak in such "stereotypical" terms (knowing he did not hear much of it), I probed at an opportune moment into why he was feeling that way.

"How dare you say that I am one of them," he almost shouted with tears in his eyes, "when my wife and I have given up all our material goods in order to be in solidarity with the poor? We have given up our privileges and power as whites in order to live with the poor and work for the poor. How could you say all whites are the same? I am not one of them!" As he spoke, I got in touch with his frustration and feeling of being rejected by the people of color in the conference. I affirmed his willingness to be in solidarity with the poor as courageous and admirable. I also invited him to reflect on the cause of people of color's reaction to him. He walked away still angry. I thought to myself that while he believed intellectually that he was in solidarity with the poor, his behavior, governed by his perception of his power, certainly did not. His individualism, his yearning to be accepted, overpowered those who did not have a strong sense of their own power. I believe it was this overpowering behavior that the people of color rejected, not his good intentions to be in solidarity with the powerless and the poor.

Good intentions are not going to create a just community. Addressing the cultural clash that is happening at an internal unconscious level will at least begin to move in that direction. The different perceptions of power among cultures are the undercurrents that drive an intercultural encounter toward "the wolf and the lamb" scenario. When we uncover these undercurrents, we will be able to work with it and redirect it so that power may be redistributed justly.

Having grown up in Hong Kong and immigrated to the United States at the age of fourteen, I spent a lot of time feeling totally powerless. When someone mistreated me, I did not fight back. When I was told to do something that I did not want to do, I did not complain. This was normal in my cultural upbringing. In Hong Kong, you began life being powerless and you waited until it was your turn to have power. You gained power in two ways: by seniority, or when an authoritative figure appointed you. Therefore, in addition to feeling powerless, I also spent a lot of time waiting to be invited to take on leadership.

I was not aware of my powerless posture until I entered the education system in the United States. Before, I waited for the teacher to recognize my worth because a teacher was expected to know every student's ability. In the States, I had to volunteer my answer to prove that I knew it better than the others. If I did not do that, the teacher might not know that I existed. It was a slow and painful process to survive the education system here. Since I was not aware of my weak sense of personal power, I constantly felt ignored by my teachers and peers. I spent many afternoons walking home after school reciting this under my breath: "How could they not know that I can do better than the others? Why did my teacher never call on me? What's wrong with me? There must be something wrong with me. I'll show them. I'll show them I am smarter next time." When the next time came, I would be frozen and powerless and not able to speak up like my other classmates. I wrote this poem in my tenth grade English class.

> I
> Timid, ambitious
> Always blaming myself
> I

What happened to me? I was living in two incompatible cultural understandings of personal power. At home and in Hong Kong, I was taught to compete. When I succeeded, I waited to be recognized. The understanding was that when I was good, others would know it and I did not need to blow my own horn, which would be considered very impolite. In order for this cultural system to work, the people in power also had the sensitivity to recognize and perceive nonverbally what people were good at and when they were ready to participate. In school in the United States, I was also taught to compete. The difference was that I had to let others know I was good or they would not notice. I did not have the awareness to see this cause of my frustration. So I thought there was something wrong with me. I blamed it on myself, which is a tendency of a powerless person. In order for me to survive school and work, I, at one point in my life, rejected my Chinese heritage, thinking that it was useless. All it did was to slow me down. If I were to climb the ladder of the American dream, I had to learn the aggressive ways of the system here.

My experience of personal power has gone through many evolutions. Through my experience of the Gospel, I learned about empowerment. I was liberated and was able to confront anything that came my way. I would never have been able to make it through seminary had I not felt that empowerment. Then during my field education with Chinese refugees from Vietnam and Cambodia, I discovered I was so overpowering that it was counterproductive. The foundations of my perception of personal power were shaken once again. I had to rethink what empowerment meant if my own empowerment could cause others to become powerless. True empowerment should empower others at the same time.

Understanding my own perception of power came into crystal-clear focus when I was doing research in multicultural ministry during my sabbatical in 1989. I read the work of Geert Hofstede. In his book, *Culture's Consequences: International Differences in Work-Related Values*, Hofstede reported the results of a research project that involved exploring "the differences in thinking and social action that exist between members of forty different modern nations." He identified "four main dimensions along which dominant value systems in the forty countries can be ordered and which affect human thinking, organizations, and institutions in predictable ways."[1] One of the dimensions, called "Power Distance," described the different understandings of inequality across cultures.

Societies in different cultures have developed different solutions to inequality. Power Distance is defined as "the extent to which the less powerful members of institutions and organizations accept that power is distributed unequally."[2] Hofstede describes this variable as a continuum, and the forty countries in which he did the survey fall somewhere in between the two extremes. One end Hofstede called the "High Power Distance" cultures, in which people believe that there should be an order of inequality in the world. In these cultures, everyone has his or her rightful place. The existence of inequality and hierarchy is an accepted fact of life. In this hierarchy, superiors and subordinates treat each other as different kinds and tend not to mix socially. On an individual level, the small elite powerholders believe that they are entitled to privileges and should try to look as powerful as possible. The powerless, which is the majority, accept their state of powerlessness and usually do not feel that they can change the system. Power and authority are usually not challenged and the legitimacy of the use of power is irrelevant. If changes are to happen to the social system, it usually happens by dethroning those in power. People in these cultures find strength and power in larger groupings. Many social changes in these societies may happen when the powerless gather together to express their dissatisfaction, which may lead toward dethroning those in power. Even though cooperation among the powerless is a way of changing the system, cooperation is very difficult to bring about because of the low level of trust among people in general. These cultures tend to have no—or a very small—

_____

[1]Geert Hofstede, *Culture's Consequences—International Differences in Work-Related Values*, abridged edition (Beverly Hills, London, New Delhi: Sage Publications,1987), p.11.

[2]G. Hofstede and M. Bond, "Hofstede's culture dimensions: An independent validation using Rokeach's value survey," *Journal of Cross-Cultural Psychology*, 15 (1984): p.419.

middle class. The majority of the people are poor and have limited access to higher education. The elite powerholders tend to be the ones who have the education and wealth.

At the other extreme, which Hofstede called "Low Power Distance," the majority of people believe that inequality in society should be minimized. The existence of a hierarchy is only for the convenience of accomplishing tasks of the organization. This inequality of roles should not affect relationships outside the organization. Superiors and subordinates treat each other as equals. People should have equal rights. People in power should try to look less powerful than they are. They spend a lot of time justifying and legitimizing their use of power. Since these cultures place importance on rewards, and legitimate and expert power, people believe that they can gain more power by doing the "right" things so that they can be rewarded with more power. They can also gain more power through education, which certifies them as experts. Implicit in this view of power is that people believe they can change the system by redistributing power. For the powerless, this means gaining more power themselves and therefore getting into the power system, forcing the system to change. For the powerful, this means including the powerless in the system by giving them power. In such a society, there is a well-developed middle class in which people reach a certain level of education. There is a minority of less-educated and low-income people in these societies that shares a belief with the majority of the people on the other end of the continuum. That belief is: they do not have any power to change the system, and they accept inequality as a given in life.[3]

Figure 2.1 (on facing page) gives a visual representation of the difference between High and Low Power Distance cultures. The triangle and rectangle represent the total population of a society. The shaded areas represent the proportion of people who believe they have power and the clear

---

[3]For a full description of High and Low Power Distance, see Hofstede, *Culture's Consequences—International Differences in Work-Related Values*, abridged edition, pp. 65–109.

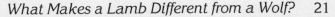

## Figure 2.1

Graphic Representation of High and Low Power Distance Cultures

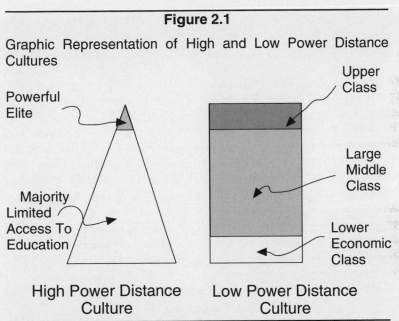

High Power Distance Culture

Low Power Distance Culture

areas represent the proportion of people who do not believe they have power. The major difference between the two cultures is that in the Low Power Distance culture there are more people who believe they have power. They are the expanded middle class. Power Distance is not only a cultural variable, but it is also a variable based on economic classes and education.

Hofstede's research data helped me understand my experience growing up in Hong Kong, which is a High Power Distance culture. By immigrating to the United States, I was thrown into a Low Power Distance culture. In my struggle to survive this culture shock, I reacted by denying my Chinese cultural heritage and tried to assimilate into the Low Power Distance culture of the United States. Then I found out that the cultural values I adopted did not prepare me for my ministry with the first-generation Chinese-American community, which maintained its High Power Distance culture. My adopted Low Power Distance cultural value was too overpowering to the High Power Distance community. Even though I set out to empower others, I was doing the opposite because of my power perception of myself.

Whenever I try to explain Hofstede's concept of Power Distance, my audience becomes confused about the terms High and Low Power Distance. One way to lessen the confusion is to see that Power Distance is inversely related to people's perception of power. That is, in a High Power Distance culture, the majority of the people believe that they have little power to change their environment of inequality. The small elite group who has the power and authority is rarely challenged. In a Low Power Distance culture, the majority of people believe that they have power to change the social system. They are not afraid to challenge authority figures and work toward a more even redistribution of power. Figure 2.2 shows countries that fall within the two ends of the Power Distance continuum.

---

### Figure 2.2

High and Low Power Distance Countries from Hofstede data

| High Power Distance | Low Power Distance |
|---|---|
| Philippines | Austria |
| Mexico | Israel |
| Venezuela | Denmark |
| India | New Zealand |
| Singapore | Ireland |
| Brazil | Sweden |
| Hong Kong | Norway |
| France | Finland |
| Colombia | Switzerland |
| Turkey | Great Britain |
| Belgium | Germany |
| Peru | Australia |
| Thailand | Netherlands |
| Chile | Canada |
| | U.S.A. |

---

The two lists illustrate that the countries in which the majority of people feel powerless are mostly Latin American and Asian countries. On the other extreme, the countries in which people feel they have power are English-speaking and Germanic language-based countries; most of these are northern European countries.

Taking this data and applying it to the multicultural situation in the United States, I hope to explain why there is a dichotomy between the people of color and whites in their perception of power in the United States. There are three factors that we have to consider:

1. The majority of recent immigrants in the United States are from Latin American and Asian countries. Recent immigrants are less influenced by the dominant culture of the United States, which believes that everyone should be equal. In other words, they tend to retain the cultural values they brought with them.

2. From a class perspective, the majority of the lower-income and less-educated people in the United States are people of color and recent immigrants. As I mentioned earlier, the low-income and less-educated class in Low Power Distance cultures behaves just like the majority of the High Power Distance culture: they believe they do not have power to change their environment.

3. Even though they have been in the United States for more than three generations and have attained the education and income level to be classified as middle-class Americans, many people of color may still retain a lot of the High Power Distance cultural traits. Their attitudes toward power may still be very different from the white middle class. This is because the melting-pot theory does not work

for people of color in the United States. The second- and third-generation European Americans can "melt" into the dominant American culture fairly easily. In many families, they are discouraged from retaining their European identities in order not to distinguish themselves from others. However, the picture is very different for immigrants of color. I was in a conference in which a Chinese American shared that she was a sixth-generation American and people continued to ask her which Asian country she was from. No matter how hard people of color try to "melt," they are not yet accepted by whites as true Americans. So the melting-pot theory works only for European Americans and it has never worked for people of color. Many people of color choose to remain in their own ethnic community for survival. In this return to isolation, even though many are more than third-generation Americans, they still retain many of their ethnic cultural values and are less affected by the dominant culture of the United States.

Putting all this together, when we are in an intercultural encounter, we can generalize that people of color tend to function like those from High Power Distance cultures. That is, they do not have a strong sense of personal power. On the other hand, white middle- and upper-class people tend to function in a Low Power Distance perception of their own power. This is confirmed by my experience of working with multicultural groups. Most of the time, white persons in the group tend to behave as if they are equal to each other and people of color tend to behave as if they are powerless.

We can see how the technical terms *High and Low Power Distance* can get in the way of my trying to explain and describe what I am trying to communicate. Instead of using these terms to represent groups with different power perceptions, I will simplify with *people of color* and *white*. I have been using these two terms loosely up to this point. With the discussion in this chapter, I will now define them more specifically. I will use the term *people of color* to represent Asian Americans, Latinos/Latinas, African Americans, and American Indians, believing that most of the time, in a multicultural situation, these groups tend to behave in a High Power Distance understanding of their personal power.

I added American Indians to the list knowing that I do not have any hard research data to back this up. I know the term *American Indian* includes many tribes and cultures, just as *Asian American* includes an even more diverse group of cultures and races. From my experience, however, whenever American Indians are involved in a multicultural group, they tend to behave in the same way as the others in this category. I believe this may have to do with their economic status.

I will use the term *whites* to represent white middle- and upper-class Americans with northern European backgrounds, believing that most of the time, in a multicultural situation, these groups tend to behave in a Low Power Distance understanding of their personal power. I recognize the danger of overgeneralization. I believe that having understood these generalized principles, we can then step back and acknowledge that, independent of people's ethnic backgrounds, they may or may not fit into this theory. The generalization is no more than a guideline or a pointer for us to analyze and reflect on our intercultural encounters. Let me tell an ancient Chinese story that illustrates this important point.

> There was a fool who wanted to buy a pair of new shoes. In preparation for this, he cut a piece of straw that measured the length of his foot. The fool thought to himself, "This would be the size of my shoes." He left his house and walked to town, which was a three-hour walk. He entered the only shoe store in town. The owner asked him, "May I help you?"
>
> "I would like to buy a pair of shoes," the fool replied.

"What size?"

At that point, the fool reached into his pocket and discovered that in his hurry to leave his house, he had left the piece of straw behind. Without another word, he ran out of the shoe store, ran all the way back home, found the piece of straw, and ran back to town. By the time he reached the shoe store, it was evening and the store was closed for the day.

As a result, the fool ran around all day without getting his new shoes.

Why did he run around looking for a piece of straw when he had his own feet right there at the store? That is why he was a fool. The model and theory that I presented in this chapter is no more than the straw that approximates the reality of how cultures might be different from each other. They are useful to us only as an instrument to help us reflect and analyze our intercultural experiences. They should not be used to make gross generalizations that further stereo-type people. That would be like the fool running around looking for straw, forgetting that he had his own feet there. One of the common mistakes that people make when they deal with models and theories is that they treat them as modes into which people have to fit. Most theories come from human experience, not human experiences from theories. Theories and models are but artificial one-dimensional rul-ers (straw) that people create to measure or try to make sense of human experiences that are multidimensional (feet). As we explore and understand more and more about the experience we try to measure or make sense of, these straws will eventually cease to represent the reality. Then theories and models need to be modified or new ones need to be developed. For now, Hofstede's High and Low Power Distance helps me understand the power dynamic between whites and people of color in the United States. I am sure that the generalization I am making will be modified and expanded as we encounter the reality of multicultural interaction.

One can say that this kind of power dynamic does not manifest itself only through cultural differences. It can occur between genders, the able and disabled, lesbian/gay and heterosexual, and the rich and poor. However, in the United States, the power dynamic set up by cultural differences is much more prominent as compared to other kinds of power differences. We need to be careful not to water down the cultural differences by lumping them together with gender and economic differences. While I must not lose sight of these other differences, my experience indicates to me that cultural differences tend to overshadow gender and economic differences in this power continuum. I will explain this further in Chapter Six.

When whites and people of color recognize that there are cultural differences in their perceptions of power, they take the first step toward doing justice. We can see that because of cultural difference some people are perceived as lions and wolves and some as lambs and calves. Furthermore, these perceptions are most likely unconscious. These perceptions set up an uneven distribution of power before the groups even meet. If the church is to become the holy mountain on which people from diverse cultures shall not hurt or destroy each other, we must respond to the call to do justice. Doing justice in a multicultural environment requires us to understand the consequences of these cultural differences in power perceptions. Doing justice commands us to reveal this unconscious and disproportionate distribution of power. Doing justice compels us to develop new leadership skills that can confront injustice. Then we can create a just community when people from different cultures encounter each other with equal strength. In the following chapters, we will explore these topics both theologically and practically. Perhaps they will contribute to the church's effort to realize the Peaceable Realm.

# CHAPTER 3

# *Differences in the Perception of Power and Their Consequences for Leadership*

In the last chapter, I made the generalization that people of color tend to perceive themselves as powerless and whites tend to perceive themselves as powerful. It is very important to recognize that this perception of power is a continuum along which people from all cultural backgrounds fall. All I am saying is that on the powerful end there is a higher concentration of whites and on the powerless end there is a higher concentration of people of color. Cultural differences, social prejudice, economic factors, and education all play a part in creating this dichotomy in the United States.

29

The consequences of this difference in perceptions of power are many. It affects communication, work relationships, family structures, and our education system, just to name a few. In other words, it affects all aspects of our society. In this book, I would like to concentrate on leadership styles and group dynamics. The definition of a leader is not the same in different cultures because how a person is expected to manage a group is dependent on the group members' perceptions of their own power. How do you lead a group of people who believe they are equal to you? How do you lead a group of people who defer to you for all the decision making because you are the authority figure? How do you lead a group of people whose perception of their power spreads from one end of the power perception continuum to the other? These are important questions to answer if the church is to raise up leaders who are able to build faithful communities in the midst of a multicultural society.

I learned in seminary how to work with groups. The seminary I attended provided a predominantly white, English-speaking environment. Therefore, the group process I learned was based on the cultural assumptions and values of the white, English-speaking middle class. Take leading a Bible study group as an example. The method I learned involved asking a series of questions coupled with an experiential exercise. The purpose of the exercise was to help the group delve deeper into the meaning of the text. I did not realize how culture-bound this method was until I facilitated a Bible study group for a Chinese-speaking group. Everything I learned about group process and facilitation of dialogue around scripture did not work. I would ask a question and the response was always a painful silence. I would ask for volunteers to participate in an experiential exercise. No one would volunteer. As a result, I ended up doing all the talking to explain what the text meant to me.

I discovered another problem with my leadership style when I encountered multicultural groups. The white members of the group would disclose their insights and thoughts verbally and freely while the people of color would just sit and listen. The more I tried to include them, the worse it got.

These experiences forced me to explore new models of leadership that took into account cultural differences and how they could affect the way we relate to each other in a multicultural group.

Depending on the cultural contexts, a group's expectation from the leadership could be very different. Leading or facilitating a group has to do with power—power to influence others and being aware of the power dynamic among the group members. Therefore, it is very important for a group leader first to determine where he or she is in the power perception continuum. How does it influence the way she behaves and interacts with others? What assumptions and expectations does he bring to the group?

Secondly, when the group leader is in a multicultural situation, there is a need to know where the people are on this power continuum. If all participants have a strong sense of their own individual power, then everything learned in white middle-class group processing would be helpful here because everyone believes that he or she is equal to everyone else unless there are "experts" in the room. A good leader is someone who enables the group to do what it needs to accomplish. People are expected to volunteer their thoughts, feelings, and talents. Differences of opinion are debated verbally. A good leader attempts to get consensus from the group. Decisions can be made by compromising. When a consensus or compromise cannot be reached, decisions fall back on voting. Robert's Rules of Order is a prime example of group process based on these assumptions. Voting, when it is not unanimous, presumes that there are winners and losers. Groups with these kinds of assumptions automatically set up a competitive environment.

An image of a good leader in a white group is a pre-traffic-lights traffic cop who stands on a platform in the middle of an intersection. His or her job is to keep all the self-moving autonomous individuals from colliding with each other. The worst of the leaders in this setting is someone who sits back and lets people fight and escalate the conflict, all in the name of democracy and respect for individual opinion and freedom. Then when things get out of hand, the leader comes in with his or her own agenda and says, "See, I gave you the power to decide and you can't seem to be able to do it. So why don't you let me decide for you?"

If everyone in the group falls on the other end of the power continuum (that is, they have a fragile sense of their individual power and would not challenge authority), someone will have to take charge and be the authoritative figure. The authoritative figure is usually the designated leader of the group. If no one takes on this role, nothing will get done. A good leader is sensitive to the needs and talents of everyone in the group. An image of a good leader is an octopus who has its tentacles extended into the different parts of the community. This person has a network of trusted people who give him or her information about what the community wants, who wishes to participate, and who has the gifts to fulfill the tasks. This person spends a lot of time before a meeting to acquire the essential information. At the meeting, the concept of invitation becomes very important because no one will volunteer. The leader has to invite people directly to offer their ideas and services. The leader will have difficulty if there are power struggles between two or more persons who believe they all have authority in the group. The worst of the leaders in this kind of group are those who use their power to push their own agenda because in such a group no one will challenge their authority.

What happens when you have a mixed group—say, one half is white and the other half is people of color? Remember that this does not happen just in a culturally mixed group; it also can happen in a mixed class group. Whenever I am in such a group, I usually observe the following pattern:

## White Group

White group members participate as they always do, and talk when they have something to say. If they disagree with someone, they disagree with them verbally and openly. Pretty soon, they realize some others are not speaking. So, with all good intentions, they try to include them by giving subtle hints because it is not considered polite to put people on the spot. It usually comes out like this: "I think everyone should jump into the discussion, if you have something to say; there is no need to be shy about it." The more they try, the more the people of color close up. As a result, they make decisions without the input and concordance of the people of color members, even though they appear to have consented to it. Then, the people of color get blamed for not participating. Occasionally, some white members feel guilty about dominating the group once more.

## People of Color Group

People of color take part in the group by expecting an authoritative leader to tell them what will happen and what to do. Instead, they hear many people talking without being invited to speak first. The assumption then is that these people must have a great deal of power and authority; so they let them talk and do not challenge them. Then, the white members of the group start hinting that they should be talking also but without a direct invitation. This may be what was going on in their minds: "If they really want my opinion, why don't they come out and ask me? Apparently, I am not smart enough," or, "How can I speak when there isn't any time to think about what I want to say?" As time goes on, they feel more and more inadequate. "And then they made decisions without asking me to contribute or do anything—I must be worthless." When the meeting ends, they leave and refuse to come back again.

What happens is that the white members of the group, by behaving "naturally" according to their cultural upbringing, are being perceived as superior by the people of color and, therefore, are given power over them. The people of color, by seeing the situation from their cultural point of view, do not know that they are perceived by the whites as equal partners in the group. The lack of understanding of this difference in the perception of power, on both sides, leads to a situation of injustice. The white group has more power than the other by controlling the agenda and decision making and unintentionally excluding the people of color. This is not the fault of any group involved. Members of the two groups, by being themselves, create a power dynamic that is like putting wolves and lambs together in one room. Something bad is going to happen because of the different "natures" of the two groups.

In an ethnocentric way, most whites believe that inequality can be countered by simply physically including the powerless and the disadvantaged. They think that by inviting an individual representative from the powerless group to join them, they are able to redistribute power more evenly. The assumption is that everyone is equal to each other as individuals and everyone is expected to participate "fully"— meaning being able to speak for himself or herself. The truth is that not all believe they are equal to each other. I have already explained why this is. Another reality is that not everyone is an individual who can speak for himself or herself. Many people of color come from cultures that emphasize the collective over the individual.[1] It is very hard for them to speak as individuals. They feel powerless without their community behind them. This explains why tokenism doesn't work. Inviting only one representative strips the power of the person by not including a collective group from which he or she comes. This is a typical response when a church organization is confronted with not having the "proper" ethnic representations: "We invited them; they came once and didn't participate. Then they stopped coming. Can't say we didn't try!"

---

[1] For a detailed discussion on individualism/collectivism, read Geert Hofstede, *Culture's Consequences—International Differences in Work-Related Values*, abridged edition (Beverly Hills, London, New Delhi: Sage Publications, 1987), pp.148–175.

This approach is what I call the ethnocentric way of doing justice. Ethnocentricism assumes one's culture is the only and superior way. With it comes the assumption that everyone should be and is like me. For whites, this means assuming everyone is equal to me in his or her power perception. Doing justice is very simple. We need only to physically include the excluded. The assumption is that once they are there they can play the power game just like us. This kind of approach to racial injustice is typical not only in churches; it also appears in the political and economic arenas of our society. Busing in the early seventies was based on this ethnocentric way of doing justice. With this assumption, we transported a small group of black students to a white school, believing that physical inclusion would take care of the problem of racial injustice. Contrary to what people expected, this kind of action actually created more unjust situations such as the one I have described.

Justice in a multicultural setting has to be approached in an "ethnorelative" way.[2] We begin by accepting the reality that people's power perceptions are different because of cultural differences. By analyzing these power perceptions and how they are relative to each other, we will see that there is a great disparity of power between the two groups. Based on this knowledge, we need to create an environment that allows people to interact with equal power and therefore redistributes power evenly. In other words, white members of the group need to know that they are perceived as powerful right from the start of the interaction and need to give up power in order to make themselves truly equal to others. People of color need to know that they are valued as equals and need to find ways to gather together a critical mass so that they can speak with power and as a collective.

In a multicultural community, we can no longer train leaders ethnocentrically. We can no longer assume every-

---

[2]The term *ethnorelative* was used by Milton J. Bennett to describe the latter three stages of intercultural sensitivity. Bennett, "Towards Ethnorelativism: A Developmental Model of Intercultural Sensitivity," in *Cross-Cultural Orientation: New Conceptualization and Application*, ed. by R. Michael Paige (University Press of America, 1986), pp.27–69.

one is like us in their power perception. We can no longer do justice by simple physical inclusion. We must move from our ethnocentric way to an ethnorelative way of doing justice. We must train leaders to be more culturally sensitive, especially to their own sense of power and how they are different from people with different cultural backgrounds. We must train leaders to do power analysis based on their cultural sensitivity. Only in this way can we be truly inclusive. Only in this way can we move from mono-cultural leadership to multicultural leadership.

In the following chapters, I shall address the injustice created by the difference in power perceptions. I shall do this first theologically through studying the scriptures. Then I will explore practical ways of addressing the issue through case study and new designs of group processes.

# CHAPTER 4

# What Does the Bible Say to the Powerful and the Powerless?

I have thus far stated the problem created by cultural differences in power perceptions between whites and people of color. In a multicultural situation, most of the time, white members of the group are perceived to be the powerful ones and people of color the powerless. I am in no way saying people of color are always powerless nor are whites always powerful. I am simply pointing out that wherever there is interaction among whites and people of color, and if members of the group are not aware of this cultural difference, the kind of power dynamic described above exists. This chapter explores what the scriptures say about inequality of power, privilege, and prestige. How does salvation come for the rich and powerful and for the poor, oppressed, and powerless? Is there a difference between how the powerful and the powerless interact with the Gospel? I hope that by exploring these issues, we can begin to do some theological reflection on this intercultural power dynamic and how we, as Christians, can address this issue productively and faithfully.

The following biblical quotations provide examples of how Jesus addressed inequality in his time.

> And [Jesus] lifted up his eyes on his disciples and said: "Blessed are you poor, for yours is the kingdom of God. Blessed are you that hunger now, for you shall be satisfied. Blessed are you that weep now, for you shall laugh....But woe to you that are rich, for you have received your consolation. Woe to you that are full now, for you shall hunger. Woe to you that laugh now, for you shall mourn and weep. Woe to you, when all speak well of you, for so their fathers did to the false prophets."
>
> Luke 6:20–26, RSV

Using folklore, Luke recorded the following parable to deepen the meaning of the passage above using images of the afterlife.

> "There was a rich man, who was clothed in purple and fine linen and who feasted sumptuously every day. And at his gate lay a poor man named Lazarus, full of sores, who desired to be fed with what fell from the rich man's table; moreover the dogs came and licked his sores. The poor man died and was carried by the angels to Abraham's bosom. The rich man also died and was buried; and in Hades, being in torment, he lifted up his eyes, and saw Abraham far off and Lazarus in his bosom. And he called out, 'Father Abraham, have mercy upon me, and send

Lazarus to dip the end of his finger in water and cool my tongue; for I am in anguish in this flame.'

But Abraham said, 'Son, remember that you in your lifetime received your good things, and Lazarus in like manner evil things; but now he is comforted here, and you are in anguish. And besides all this, between us and you a great chasm has been fixed, in order that those who would pass from here to you may not be able, and no one may cross from there to us.'

And he said, 'Then I beg you, father, to send him to my father's house, for I have five brothers, so that he may warn them, lest they also come into this place of torment.' But Abraham said, 'They have Moses and the prophets; let them hear them.' And he said, 'No, father Abraham; but if someone goes to them from the dead, they will repent.' He said to him, 'If they do not hear Moses and the prophets, neither will they be convinced if some one should rise from the dead.'"

Luke 16:19–30, RSV

What can a rich and powerful person do to undo this predicament? The following was what Jesus told a ruler who came to ask him, "What shall I do to inherit eternal life?" (Luke 18:18).

Jesus said to him, "One thing you still lack. Sell all that you have and distribute to the poor, and you will have treasure in heaven; and come, follow me." But when he heard this he became sad, for he was very rich.

Luke 18:22–23, RSV

Notice the contrast between how the poor and the rich were addressed. Those who had prestige, wealth, and power were cursed. They also had the additional responsibility of giving up and redistributing their wealth and power. But the poor and oppressed did not have to do anything. They were simply blessed. All that was required of them was righteousness, endurance, and faithfulness.

> Love the LORD, all you his saints!
>     The LORD preserves the faithful,
>     but abundantly requites him who acts haughtily.
> Be strong, and let your heart take courage,
>     all you who wait for the LORD!
>
> Psalm 31:23–24, RSV

The scribes and the Pharisees were people with power and prestige in the Jewish community. The following was what Jesus said concerning them:

> "The scribes and the Pharisees sit on Moses' seat; so practice and observe whatever they tell you, but not what they do; for they preach, but do not practice. They bind heavy burdens, hard to bear, and lay them on men's shoulders; but they themselves will not move them with their finger. They do all their deeds to be seen by men; for they make their phylacteries broad and their fringes long, and they love the place of honor at feasts and the best seats in the synagogues, and salutations in the market places, and being called rabbi by men. But you are not to be called rabbi, for you have one teacher, and you are all brethren. And call no man your father on earth, for you have one Father, who is in heaven. Neither be called masters, for you have one master, the Christ. He who is greatest among you shall be your servant; whoever exalts himself will be humbled, and whoever humbles himself will be exalted.
>
> Matthew 23:1–12, RSV

Here Jesus went even further in saying that those who serve and humble themselves are the greatest. This was the opposite of what being great and honored meant in most societies. This passage also pointed out that in the community of Christ, there was to be even distribution of power among people. The only one who had more power was God in heaven. Even so, God became human through Jesus Christ, who exemplified greatness in serving and in being powerless on the cross.

In the Judeo-Christian tradition, the attitude toward the powerful and rich is very different from the attitude toward the poor and the powerless. The powerful in society are challenged to give up their power and wealth and redistribute it in order to achieve equality among the people of God. To the powerful, the emphasis is on serving and being humble. The powerful are judged by God for their use of their power and privilege. In some places in Scripture, the powerful are actually put down. "...It is easier for a camel to go through the eye of a needle than for someone who is rich to enter the kingdom of God" (Matthew 19:24).

The powerless, however, are lifted up, cared for and loved by God because of their faithfulness. To the powerless, the emphasis is on endurance and faithfulness. God has compassion on those who are oppressed and suffering. They are loved by God even though they have no worldly goods and power. They are blessed even though they are suffering now. The powerless are powerful in God's sight even though they are oppressed now. God will deliver them from all this. "Do not be afraid, stand firm, and see the deliverance that the LORD will accomplish for you today;...The LORD will fight for you, and you have only to keep still" (Exodus 14:13–14).

This difference in attitude toward the powerful and the powerless was very clear throughout the ministry of Jesus. Jesus never told the poor and powerless to sell all they own and give to the poor. That would obviously be an absurd thing to say. Jesus healed them, loved them, ate with them, touched them, comforted them, blessed them, served them, encouraged them, taught them, and liberated them by his own suffering, death, and resurrection. Finally, Jesus breathed on them to infuse them with the power of the Holy Spirit—the power to teach, heal, and forgive in the name of God. On the other hand, Jesus never told the rich and powerful that they are blessed. Instead, Jesus warned them and challenged them to serve and to humble themselves. He reminded them of what the law and the prophets had said.

The Gospel invites the powerful to take up their cross and follow Jesus. Salvation for the powerful comes from the decision to give up power and take up the cross. The Gospel, however, never asks the powerless to choose the cross because the powerless, by their condition of power-lessness, are already on the cross. There is no need for them to choose it, just as there is no need for the poor to give up what they have and give to the poor because they are already poor. Because the powerless are already on the cross, salvation comes from endurance and faithfulness in the hope of God's deliverance through the resurrection.

Choosing the cross and the resurrection of Jesus are part of the same Gospel story. But we interact with the different parts of the story differently depending on our place of power in a particular situation. As a Chinese American working in the Episcopal Church, I often find myself in situations where I am set up to be powerless. For example, I am sometimes invited to be the token Asian in a meeting. When I am in this kind of situation, I actually spend time before I enter the meeting to get in touch with the empty tomb, the resurrection side of the Gospel. I tell myself that I am blessed and a child of God no matter what happens. I ask God to breathe the Holy Spirit through me to give me strength to endure and power to speak and challenge the system I am about to enter.

On the other hand, as a trainer and consultant I also find myself in situations where I am given power and authority to influence others. In my preparation for each training ses-sion, I spend time reflecting on what it means to choose the cross. I tell myself that I am a servant to the participants. I tell myself that even though I may be treated as an expert, I must be humble. I tell myself that my job is to work myself out of my job by giving my knowledge, skills, and power away freely, so that at the end of the session, the partici-pants will know what I know and my services are no longer needed.

It is crucial to determine in a given situation which side of the cross we are on if we are to experience the wholeness of the Gospel. No one can stay on one side of the cross all the time. That would be neglecting the wholeness of the Gospel. Living the Gospel involves moving through the cycle of death and resurrection, the cross and the empty tomb, again and again. The moment I am resurrected into new life of empowerment, I must begin to think about serving and giving away my power and take up the cross again, or I stand the chance of abusing my power. The moment I take up the cross and become powerless, I must begin to think about faithfulness and endurance and look toward empowerment through the empty tomb. It is in this dynamic of death and resurrection, cross and the empty tomb, Lent and Easter, that the Gospel comes to life in each one of us.

In the previous chapter, we exposed the injustice created by cultural difference in power perceptions among different cultural groups. In a multicultural encounter, the whites tend to become too powerful and the people of color powerless. Therefore, it is imperative that we understand how our biblical tradition addresses the powerful and the powerless. In this chapter, we discovered that the Gospel commands the powerful to give up power and the powerless to endure and be faithful. Furthermore, the Gospel story empowers the powerless to take up power to do the mighty work of God. In the following chapters, we will further explore how these Gospel imperatives are practiced in our lives.

# CHAPTER 5

# A Fresh Look at Pentecost as the Beginning of a Multicultural Church Community

When the day of Pentecost had come, they were all together in one place. And suddenly a sound came from heaven like the rush of a mighty wind, and it filled all the house where they were sitting. And there appeared to them tongues as of fire, distributed and resting on each one of them. And they were all filled with the Holy Spirit and began to speak in other tongues, as the Spirit gave them utterance.

Now there were dwelling in Jerusalem Jews, devout men from every nation under heaven. And at this sound the multitude came together, and they were bewildered, because each one heard them speaking in his own language. And they were amazed and wondered, saying, "Are not all these who are speaking Galileans? And how is it that we hear, each of us in his own native language? Parthians and Medes and Elamites and residents of Mesopotamia, Judea and Cappadocia, Pontus and Asia, Phrygia and Pamphylia, Egypt and the parts of Libya belonging to Cyrene, and visitors from Rome, both Jews and proselytes, Cretans and Arabians, we hear them telling in our own tongues the mighty works of God."

Acts 2:1–11, RSV

Pentecost, which marked the beginning of the church, provided the ideal image of how people from different cultural backgrounds should be able to live together. With the power of the Holy Spirit, they could understand each other in this miracle of communication. The church ever since Pentecost has strived for this ideal but never quite accomplished it. I had read and heard the Pentecost story interpreted to me many times ever since I was a child—first in Roman Catholic primary school in Hong Kong, then in the Episcopal Church in New York's Chinatown, and then in college campus ministry. The Pentecost story was always explained to me as the miracle of the tongues—that is, the Holy Spirit gave the disciples the power to speak in different languages in order to communicate the "mighty works of God." As the youngest child in a Chinese family, I certainly did not believe I had that gift. As a teenager in the United States, trying desperately to learn English, I was certain that I did not have the gift of tongues. Even in seminary, I had not heard the Pentecost miracle interpreted as anything other than that of a miracle of the tongue.

Then I went to a Bible study training conference conducted by Walter Wink and June Keener-Wink. The first question that Walter asked after reading this passage was: Is this a miracle of the tongue or is this a miracle of the ear? This simple question cracked open our ethnocentric interpretation of the Bible passage. For the first time, I was able to read and hear verses 6 and 7. The multitude knew that the disciples were speaking Galilean and yet they could understand them in their own languages. To understand the Pentecost event as exclusively a miracle of the tongue is only perceiving half of what was happening. The miracle of the tongue is more action-oriented. It involves putting out words in other tongues. It involves giving information. The miracle of the ear is more "passive." It involves listening and receiving information.

Using Pentecost as an ideal, the church in the West took the active, miracle-of-the-tongue approach. The pattern was that if you were to spread the Gospel, you must first learn to speak the language of the people with whom you were trying to communicate and then you preach to them about the "mighty works of God." This was the traditional missionary approach. History has shown us the negative results of this miracle-of-the-tongue approach. In the recent years, *missionary* became a bad word for my denomination. The Episcopal Church, in dealing with its guilt, has taken an indifferent attitude toward missions. While we do not want to be too pushy, we fall short of realizing the miracle of the ear. Instead of training whites to speak a different language, the church has raised up indigenous leaders from the various cultures to evangelize. As a result, most of the multicultural churches in the United States consisted of monolingual and most likely monocultural congregations sharing the same facility with little or no real communication or interaction among the various groups. In some situations, power struggles among the groups took shape in such questions as: "Who owns the church?" "Who are members of the church?" "Does each congregation give enough money to maintain the church?" This to me is going back to the Tower of Babel.

Another approach that also falls short of the miracle of the ear is the ethnocentric way of doing justice that is based on the naive belief that by putting two culturally very different groups together, the Holy Spirit will make Pentecost happen. This has usually happened when there is a declining white congregation in the midst of a changing neighborhood where a growing non-English-speaking congregation is using a rented facility to worship. The church authority thinks this is a perfect opportunity to enable Pentecost to happen by combining the two congregations. Financially, this would save the white congregation from having to close the church. At the same time, the growing "ethnic" congregation could have a real home. These situations usually look great on paper. The two groups literally are thrown into the situation without any intercultural sensitivity training. As a result, most of these congregations revert back to multi-congregational structure in which the different groups maintain their own worship, governance, and leadership. Even though they are all under one name and one roof, they tend to have very little interaction with each other, and when they do, there are conflicts and power struggles among them.

To realize Pentecost in our time, we must understand this miracle in its fullness. Doing a power analysis in the Pentecost situation is crucial to understanding this miracle. Power analysis, as I use it here, is nothing more than looking at who has the power and who is powerless in the social, political, and economic context of the event. Knowing this information will shed light on many situations, not only in what is recorded in the Holy Scriptures but also in our time.

The disciples, who believed Jesus was the Messiah, were part of a very small minority among the Jews. They believed Jesus' death and resurrection signified that he was the one sent by God to bring salvation to all. To the Romans, they were just another sect of Judaism whose leader had been executed. Considering these preceding events, the disciples and Jesus' other followers should be in hiding, in fear of further persecution. Instead, in their seemingly powerless state, they were given the power to speak in tongues and later to preach in authority in public places. The miracle of the tongue was the Holy Spirit's inspiration to the powerless to see that they were blessed in their weakness. In that blessedness they found strength to speak out and proclaim the mighty works of God. The miracle of the tongue was for the powerless.

On the other hand, in the Pentecost event, the "devout Jews from every nation who dwell in Jerusalem" were the powerful ones in this context. They were the ones who demanded that Pilate crucify Jesus instead of the "notorious prisoner" Barabbas. They were the majority who did not believe that Jesus was the Messiah. If they wanted, they could have handed the disciples over to the officials to be persecuted. Indeed, they were the powerful ones in this situation. Yet, they were given the miracle of the ear. They were given the gift of listening and understanding even though what was said by the disciples was in another language. They were in the receiving mode. Some still did not understand but thought they were drunk. But others were amazed. The miracle of the ear for the powerful, working together with the miracle of the tongue for the powerless, was essential to make the Pentecost experience complete.

If the church is to move toward Pentecost in the midst of a multicultural society, it must work in cooperation with the Holy Spirit to make the miracle of the tongue and the miracle of the ear happen according to the perception and reality of the power dynamics among different cultural groups in the community. This implies a bridge-building strategy that requires two different approaches from the different cultural banks. On one end, the church needs to teach the white middle and upper class to listen. The church needs to encourage those who are perceived as powerful to practice the spirituality of choosing the cross. The instinct for the powerful is to act, control, and command. The church should challenge the powerful to go against that instinct. The church should invite them to get out of the "doing" mode and enter into a "being" mode of listening. The Gospel challenges them to give up and redistribute their power to the powerless.

On the other end, the church needs to encourage people of color to gather in communities of their choosing. In these communities of faith, they are encouraged to find their identity and strength just as the powerless disciples gathered together before the Pentecost event. Then, the church needs to give them a platform to address the whole church. If the church is to respond to the yearning of the Holy Spirit, it should move toward supporting the communities of people of color to come forth and exercise the miracle of the tongue and speak of the mighty works of God. Remember that the powerless and the weak are blessed. It is through their faith together that they find power to endure and to speak the truth.

It is essential that the two approaches be taken together so that those in power and the powerless can meet in the middle where they can interact on equal ground. If the communities of color are ready to proclaim the mighty works of God, but the white members of the church are not listening but are in a doing and talking mode, nothing will change, at best. At worst, the people of color will be challenged and put down. They may get so frustrated that they will not accept another invitation to speak in a multicultural situation. The feelings may be, "Why bother! They will never listen anyway." Many of the racism workshops that I have observed in seminaries, churches, and dioceses fall under this kind of incomplete approach to multicultural encounters.

On the other hand, if whites are ready to listen but people of color are not given the time and space to build the communities of strength together, there will be nothing to which to listen. The people of color will then be blamed for not being prepared even though they were given the chance to be equal to the others. Tokenism, with all its good intention to include "minorities," is an example of this approach. Both groups need to do their homework before a true intercultural encounter can occur. Most of the time, the church makes a move before either of the communities involved is ready. As a result, the tremendous effort and excitement to realize Pentecost has been in vain.

In order for an intercultural encounter to be truly "pentecostal," the church must first value monocultural gatherings. For people of color, a monocultural gathering serves as a time to be in community, to gain self-esteem in the context of the collective, and to gain strength before moving into a world that does not value who they are. It is a time to learn that they are blessed, that in their endurance they are resurrected into the new life of empowerment. It is a time to heal, a time to gather and build up strength, a time to embrace, and a time to speak. For whites, a monocultural gathering is a time to clarify and understand what it means to be whites in this society. It serves as a time for reflection on how they have taken their power and privilege for granted. It is a time to refrain from doing and trying to "fix" the problem but a time to listen and keep silence. It is a time for repentance, a time to accept the burden of the cross, a time to break down denials, and a time to cast away stones that built and supported the foundations of the racist system. There is a lot of resistance to this kind of movement because on the surface it looks like segregation again. However, if we know the purposes of these gatherings, we will not allow permanent segregation to happen. Only after the powerful and the powerless have done their homework can they come together in a true "pentecostal" encounter.

"For everything there is a season, and a time for every matter under heaven," said the writer of Ecclesiastes (3:1). That is true. The question is, when is the right time for whom to do what? This discernment is crucial and can be accomplished only by doing power analysis on ourselves as we relate to others based on the social, political, and economic context of the situation.

# CHAPTER 6

# Who Has Power and Who Doesn't? Power Analysis, an Essential Skill for Leadership in a Multicultural Community

Then Moses stretched out his hand over the sea. The LORD drove the sea back by a strong east wind all night, and turned the sea into dry land; and the waters were divided. The Israelites went into the sea on dry ground, the waters forming a wall for them on their right and on their left. The Egyptians pursued, and went into the sea after them, all of Pharaoh's horses, chariots, and chariot drivers. At the morning watch the LORD in the pillar of fire and cloud looked down upon the Egyptian army, and threw the Egyptian army into panic. He clogged their chariot wheels so that they turned with difficulty. The Egyptians said, "Let us flee from the Israelites, for the LORD is fighting for them against Egypt."

Then the Lord said to Moses, "Stretch out your hand over the sea, so that the water may come back upon the Egyptians, upon their chariots and chariot drivers." So Moses stretched out his hand over the sea, and at dawn the sea returned to its normal depth. As the Egyptians fled before it, the LORD tossed the Egyptians into the sea. The waters returned and covered the chariots and the chariot drivers, the entire army of Pharaoh that had followed them into the sea; not one of them remained. But the Israelites walked on dry ground through the sea, the waters forming a wall for them on their right and on their left.

Exodus 14:21–29

I was in a retreat on scriptural meditation through dance. One of the leaders described the story of Exodus and asked us to identify with being in slavery. Then we were asked to create a dance that would move us from slavery into freedom. I looked around the room and saw that the majority of the group was white American. I voiced my discomfort with this proceeding. As the group discussed this further, I realized I was reacting to the inappropriateness of a group of white Americans identifying with slavery when they were perceived as being powerful by most people of color in the United States. *They should be identifying with Pharaoh and his army,* I thought. *They should be examining their privileges that they have taken for granted. They should be identifying with being soldiers of Pharaoh's army with their horses and chariots and armors and weapons. They should be getting in touch with what it meant to be affected by the plagues and to be drowned in the Red Sea.*

The story of Exodus was about God liberating the Israelites who were in slavery. The difference in power and strength between the Israelites and Pharaoh's army was apparent: the Israelites walked on foot and Pharaoh's army had chariots and horses. For the powerless Israelites, God was on their side. They were blessed and God would deliver them as long as they remained faithful to God. Out of this blessedness they were able to walk across the Red Sea on dry land. They were able to live through the ordeal of the wilderness and had strength to enter Canaan, the promised land.

Our retreat leader's request of white Americans to identify themselves exclusively with slavery was disturbing to me because it is dangerous for the powerful to identify themselves as the powerless victims. For example, the early European-American settlers suffered religious persecution in Europe. It was very understandable for them to think of America as the promised land. However, when they met the American Indians in an intercultural encounter, they were perceived as powerful people. In this situation, there was a powerful group who believed they were victims. They mistakenly believed that they had the right to claim the land as their promised land. The result was the genocide of the American Indians. This was a case of how dangerous it is for the powerful to take on the spirituality of the oppressed and the powerless. If they had realized at that point that they were perceived as powerful, then they might have identified with the powerful Pharaoh instead of the oppressed Israelites. If that had happened, the history of North America might be different.

Pharaoh and the Israelites are parts of the Exodus story. The miracle of the tongue and the ear are interrelated parts of the Pentecost story. Choosing the cross and the resurrection are parts of the same salvation story of the Gospel. Depending on the cultural contexts of the readers and the context of the multicultural situation, the same scriptural story may challenge, support, affirm, motivate, or even put down different people. In other words, if scriptural study is shared among people from different cultures, people from one cultural context will be able to hear how people from a different cultural context interact with the same scriptural story. Imagine a group having a conversation around the Exodus story in which the powerful identify with Pharaoh and the powerless identify with the Israelites. Reflection on the story will be richer as a result. Different points of view are explored. Perhaps reconciliation may begin to happen between the powerful and the powerless. In this sense, scriptural study in a multicultural community can help us see a more complete scriptural story.

Church leaders today have to understand how the Gospel speaks to the powerless and the powerful differently. They must learn when to teach them appropriately according to their application to different cultural groups. Preaching in a bilingual liturgy becomes more and more difficult as I grow in my understanding of cultural differences. The old way of translating a sermon from one language to another just does not work anymore. Maybe it never worked. When I prepared a sermon in English, I found after translating it into Chinese that the sermon became too personal and individualistic, sometimes too psychological and not action-oriented. If I prepared a sermon in Chinese first, the translation into English became too repetitive, sometimes too community-centered, and perhaps uninteresting to the English-speaking listeners. After much reflection, I realized that the thought patterns and logic I used when I was preparing an English and a Chinese sermon were very different. Not only that, the content of the sermon changed because of the audience I had in mind. I found the theme I was preaching in Chinese was leaning toward liberation. It was about taking on power and action to change the injustices of our society. The theme I was preaching in English revolved around repentance, forgiveness and giving. Now when I am asked about preaching in a bilingual liturgy, I encourage people to preach two different sermons.

Teaching a white group to bear the cross is totally appropriate in a multicultural setting. In fact, Western Christianity has emphasized this aspect of the Gospel for centuries. Most English-speaking white congregations have a very extensive Lenten program but very little Easter celebration. The white American liturgical churches seem to be obsessed with Lent. Lent is the time all the special programs begin. Lent is a time for special retreats, lectures, prayer groups, and Bible studies. The first Sunday after Easter is called low Sunday because the attendance is usually the lowest. When I asked a group of fellow Christians one time to celebrate the Good News of the risen Christ the day after Easter, the reply was, "Not today, I am too tired."

However, teaching people of color about bearing the cross first is not appropriate. That is like teaching poor persons that they have to sell all their possessions and give them to the poor. You do not have to choose the cross when you are already on the cross. Instead, we should be teaching blessedness, the empty tomb, the resurrection, and Easter celebration. In the Chinese Christian church, very little attention is given to Lent. In fact, most of the time, Lent begins around the time of the Chinese New Year celebration, which is our most joyous festival. We seem to skip Lent altogether and go straight to Easter. One of my earliest childhood memories was going to church on Easter Sunday. I loved the joyful hymns, the flowers, and the brightness of the event. In the community of my childhood, which consisted of mostly poor Chinese in Hong Kong, the emphasis was on the resurrection and not on suffering, because there was so much suffering in the community already. Liberation theology, which has its primary development in Latin America and Africa, emphasizes God's favor for the oppressed and God's plan to liberate them. Liberation theology emerges out of the kind of spirituality that emphasizes the empty tomb, the resurrection, and blessedness.

It is equally dangerous to teach people of color the theology of the cross. Many white missionaries, whose spirituality is grounded in the cross, naturally want to preach and share it in their evangelizing work. However, preaching salvation that came from choosing the cross to a group of already powerless people reinforces their perception of their powerlessness. As a result, some powerless groups actually believe that suffering is good for them and that suffering is part of their salvation.

Power analysis becomes critical if we are to live out the fullness of the Gospel. We must ask the questions: In this social, economic, and political context, who has power and who does not? Who is perceived to be powerful and who is perceived to be powerless? In a multicultural world, we might find ourselves shifting back and forth between being powerful and powerless depending on the contexts in which we relate to others. In any given situation, we must determine where we stand in relation to others in the power continuum. This determination will govern which spirituality and theology we ought to practice and teach. If I find myself in a powerless position in relation to others, I must practice the spirituality of the empty tomb. If I find myself in a powerful place, I must practice the spirituality of the cross.

To help people understand the importance of power analysis in multicultural groups, I have used a process of group division that I learned from working with the National Conference of Christians and Jews. In a typical process, I first divide the group by color—a group of whites and a group of people of color. Both groups are asked to discuss their experiences in an intercultural encounter. When the groups return, they report their findings. One question keeps surfacing in these discussions: Which group is perceived to have power? In this division, the groups agree that the white group is perceived to have more power. Then, I divide the group again by gender. They are asked to discuss their experience in inter-gender encounters. When they report back, one of the observations is that the men are perceived as powerful, and the women as powerless.

In the group divisions, the power position of white men and women of color stays the same. White men are perceived as powerful while women of color are perceived as powerless in both groupings. The emphases of their spirituality are more consistent. White men will need to practice the spirituality of the cross most of the time in a multicultural situation. However, white men do not have to choose the cross all the time. If we divide the group once again by income—a rich group and a poor group—there will be white men on both the powerful and powerless sides. But in most cases, I have found that the color division tends to be the dominant force in determining people's perceptions of their power. For women of color, liberation is the word. Most of the time, they need to practice the spirituality of the empty tomb and the resurrection in a multicultural situation. I believe very strongly that women of color need to spend time together in order to build the self-esteem and power base to challenge the system that treats them as powerless people most of the time.

White women and men of color experienced a shift in power perception in this group division process. White women are considered powerful in the first grouping because they are white in the first grouping. But as women, they are considered powerless in the second grouping. The men of color are considered powerless because they are people of color in the first grouping. In the second grouping, they are considered powerful as men. The point I want to make is that in a multicultural environment we need to be sensitive to where we are in the continuum of power perception, especially white women and men of color. Depending on the context, these two groups may be perceived as either powerful or powerless. Therefore, they need to learn to shift between practicing the spirituality of the cross and the empty tomb.

To many people, this sounds very inconsistent. Many bicultural church leaders, who can function in more than one cultural group, often are accused of being inconsistent—two-faced. Consistency seems to be one of white America's highest values. If you are not consistent in your belief, you are called "wishy-washy." Politicians running for office are being scrutinized especially for their consistency in stands on issues. They lose credibility if they are discovered to be inconsistent. Therefore, they cannot be trusted. This value of consistency can easily be transferred to our understanding of our power. If this value is not challenged, in an intercultural encounter, the group that has to shift in its power perception will not be able to adapt and conflict will most certainly arise.

For example, I was in a conference where the participants were finally at a point where they were ready for a more in-depth discussion of cultural differences. In the course of the discussion, an African American found enough courage to tell the group what it was like growing up as a person of color. Before this person finished, a white woman said that the African American's experience was no different from her own experience as a woman. Then she continued with a litany of her own experience of how she was oppressed by men all her life. The more the people of color tried to explain that there were differences, the more the white participants disagreed. They said: "What you experienced was part of what all human beings have to get through growing up, black, white, Asian, Hispanic, women, etc." This went back and forth for a few rounds and eventually the people of color got totally frustrated and retreated to silence. Here was an example of what might happen if people do not realize their power perception has changed due to the context. The white woman was right in saying that she was oppressed and powerless when compared with men. However, what she did not realize was that in the multicultural context as a white person, she is perceived as powerful. Here, consistency of her perception of her power needs to be challenged.

Seminary education for many men of color has the same effect. For example, a community of color raised up a male leader to consider the ordained ministry. In most communities of color, the leaders were greatly respected and given a lot of power. This man was probably given much authority and many leadership opportunities before he reached this point. The church sent him to seminary where, with a few exceptions, he was taught in a white middle-class, English-speaking context. In this context, he felt powerless and naturally focused his work on the spirituality of empowerment. Of course, seminary also reinforced the value of consistency. After seminary, he returned to his community to serve. But the community found him to be too powerful and insensitive. Here was an already powerful person in his own community being educated to claim even more power. No wonder he was not accepted by his own community. In addition to teaching the spirituality of empowerment in a white environment, seminary education also should have nurtured this person, who was perceived by his own community as powerful, to focus his work and spirituality on humility, servanthood, and giving power to others. Because of the shift in power perception for men of color, they need to be very careful as they move in and out of different cultural contexts.

"For everything there is a season and a time for every matter under heaven." Pharaoh and his army, Moses, and the Israelites are parts of the same Exodus story. Jesus' death on the cross and resurrection are parts of the same salvation story. Lent and Easter are seasons of the same church year. But each story begins with powerful and powerless roles. As each story is being told through the words of the Judeo-Christian storytellers, the politically powerful ones become spiritually powerless and the politically powerless ones become spiritually powerful. "...many who are first will be last, and the last will be first" (Matt. 19:30). The movement from being powerful to powerless and then from powerless to powerful is the dynamic of the Gospel. We need to know, in a given context, where our starting point is. If we find ourselves perceived as powerful, we must take on the spirituality of the cross and move toward being powerless. If we find ourselves perceived as powerless, we must take on the spirituality of resurrection and move toward being powerful. In a multicultural society, this dynamic becomes more complicated because we can shift from being powerful in one moment to being powerless in the next and vice versa. A leader in a multicultural community must learn to do power analysis on a given situation. Based on this analysis, the leader will determine his or her style of leadership, theological emphasis, and spirituality.

# CHAPTER 7

# The Wolves Lie Down with the Lambs

## A Case Study

In this chapter, we will look at a case study in which a multicultural group succeeded temporarily to live out the spirituality of choosing the cross for the white members of the group and the spirituality of resurrection for the people of color.

I was a resource person for a young adult conference. The conference planners were very intentional about recruiting participants for this conference so that there would be representatives from the various ethnic groups in the region. As a result of their effort, one third of the participants

were people of color—Japanese American, American Indian, African American, El Salvadorian American, native
Hawaiian, and Chinese American—and the other two-thirds
were European Americans.

What happened during the first two days of the conference was repeated episodes of the typical pattern described
in Chapter Three. The white members of the group did all
the talking and the people of color rarely participated verbally. It was apparent that they were very uncomfortable.
The silence was loaded with anxiety. The conference leaders tried every trick in group processing but could not get
the people of color to participate verbally. The more sensitive members of the white group tried to reach out to the
people of color. The effort to communicate with them one-
on-one was helpful, but whenever there were more than
three people in the group, they could not seem to participate.

Most of the time the whole group, about thirty people,
worked and had discussion together. For Bible study and
small-group sharing, the participants were divided into
groups of six. Since there were only about ten persons of
color, the planner followed the usual strategy of putting one
or two persons of color in each group. By the morning of the
third day, two persons of color did not show up. When
others went to look for them, they discovered that they were
not feeling well and decided to stay in their rooms. In Bible
study group that morning, two persons in two different
groups broke down and cried after being pressured by
others to speak. One of them actually said that she felt so
useless in the group that she might as well not have come.

I was invited to this conference especially to do a workshop on "Multicultural Decision Making" on the afternoon of
the third day. With the help of a friend, Ida Johnson, a black
American from the West Indies, we designed the following
process. We divided the participants into two groups: a
white group and a people of color group. They were put in
separate rooms and were given identical tasks: to evaluate
the last two days and come back with a recommendation on
the agenda for the last day of the conference.

In the white group, the first reaction was guilt. "Why are we talking about them without their being here?" "We should be including them here." After much discussion, someone finally said, "Look, we've tried everything. Nothing is working. Why don't we shut up and listen to them? Maybe that will help." Someone else began to propose a plan of how they could invite the other group to share and they would listen. Then they realized that they were doing "it" again—being the ones in control. So they decided to abandon all plans and simply went back with the agenda to listen and "to let" the other group go first.

In the people of color group, of which I was a part, I decided to take a more directive leadership style. At first, I asked them how they were doing. Their responses were standard polite ones: "I am learning a lot," "I am making many new friends," and "The people here are very nice." When I pushed further by stating the fact that they were not participating in the last two days and asked them what could be the cause of it, they began to open up. These were samples of what was shared.

> "I grew up in a traditional Hawaiian home; children were to be seen and not heard."

> "As a woman, I was taught not be speak unless I was talked to first."

> "After a while, I decided that if they had so much to say, why don't I just let them talk?"

> "This is the first time I have been in a conference like this. I came expecting to listen and learn more about the Episcopal Church. I didn't expect to be asked to talk. If I knew enough to talk about it in the group, I wouldn't need to come to the conference in the first place."

> "Everyone seems to be so smart here. I feel so bad that I could not say anything."

After more than an hour of sharing, the group decided that what they just shared was very important for the other group to hear. But they were unsure of sharing these feelings in front of the whole group. After more discussion, we decided that we would ask to go first and we would invite three of them who had been quiet in the last two days to join us in a circle in the middle of the room. Then we would invite the rest of the participants to turn around and face the wall and listen. This way, the inner circle could be free to share without a lot of people staring at them.

When we returned with everyone in same room again, I decided not to direct which group should report first. There was again a pregnant silence. The people-of-color group had elected a spokesperson, and I knew that she was trying to find enough courage to speak first. But the white group beat us to it. A white spokesperson said, "We have decided to let you go first." The people-of-color spokesperson said, "We were going to ask to go first." There was immediate relief with much laughter. The people-of-color spokesperson began by asking two questions.

"Are you willing to listen to our stories?" A resounding "Yes" was the response.

"Are you willing to take the responsibility of taking these stories home with you?" Again, the answer was yes.

The people-of-color group picked three whites who had been fairly quiet through the last two days and invited them to sit with them in a small circle in the middle of the room. The rest of the white group was asked to turn around, face the wall, and just listen in silence. The group in the middle reenacted what happened in their small-group discussion. They shared how they felt frustrated and powerless, and they talked about why they felt that way. There were many tears and emotions shared. At the end of the sharing, almost everyone was crying, including the people who faced the wall in silence all that time.

After some reflection on the experience in the large group, the whole group agreed on a new way of being together for the rest of the conference. The agreement was that for every white person who spoke, a person of color was invited to speak and vice versa. This was how it actually worked out. A white person would speak, usually at length. Then there was a silence. The quality of the silence was different this time because everyone knew that the silence was a time for thinking and courage building and mutual support. Most importantly, the silence was an invitation to a member of the people-of-color group to share. After a period, a person of color would speak, usually briefly. Immediately, a white participant would jump in. Then there was a period of silence again. Then another person of color would share briefly. Then a white person would jump in right away. I described what followed as a dance. There was a definite choreography that the group had agreed upon. Yet, there was spontaneity in the sharing. For the first time, everyone in the group was participating and sharing. The wolf and the lamb finally could dwell together peacefully.

The turning point of the situation was the physical separation of the two groups—one was perceived as powerful and the other powerless. The physical separation was merely a visual indication of the psychological and social barriers that were already there. In the process of dealing with this uncomfortable separation, the white group recognized their position of power even though they had not meant it to be that way. Their good intentions to include seemed to have the opposite effect. They realized that there was something else at work that was beyond their control. With this knowledge, they chose to take the position of the powerless—of not being in control—by asking the people of color to share first and then remain silent and listen. To be silent, to let go of control, to be passive and just "be," were not "natural" according to the white cultural values. They were taught that it was good to take charge, it was good to speak up as an individual, and it was good to be active and "do something" to correct the problem. Their choice to give up power was going against their instinct. It had to be very uncomfortable and limiting for them. Yet, that was what was required of them in order truly to accomplish what they had set out to do—to be inclusive, to treat everyone as an equal, independent of his or her culture, class, and race. There was a shift in the understanding of equality. Equality was not sameness of behavior and values. They had learned that they could not expect the other to behave the same way as they behave. Instead, equality came only after they had recognized the inequality of power and that it was through giving up of power that equality could occur.

For the people of color, the separation from the white group brought relief. For the first time, they could share what they were feeling with others who had similar experiences. In sharing their powerlessness, they found community. Through connecting with others in community, they found strength and self-esteem. They recognized that they were not alone and they were not stupid. They were just different. In this common strength, they realized that they were equal to the white group. As a collective, they too could take control of the situation. When they returned to the large group, the spokesperson spoke with power on behalf of the group. Power for most people of color comes from the collective and not the individual.

The experience of the white group in this conference was a living example of a group realizing their domination just by being who they were and deciding to take a powerless position. In this case, they literally faced the wall in order to be equal to the people of color. For the people of color, by being in a group of seemingly powerless people, they found power and self-esteem in their collectiveness and returned to meet the other on equal ground. The resolution to speak alternately was an example of creating an environment in which everyone is interacting on equal ground.

> "If [anyone] would come after me, let him deny himself and take up his cross and follow me. For whoever would save his life will lose it; and whoever loses his life for my sake and the gospel's will save it."
> Mark 8:34–35, RSV

This is what it means for white persons to do justice in a multicultural setting. Only after the decision to take the powerless position, to bear the cross, could they be resurrected to new life in the new creation where everyone is equal. On the other hand, people of color, in a multicultural setting, would not need to choose the cross because by being themselves they were powerless and, therefore, on the cross. What they needed to know was that they are blessed and would be resurrected to the new life of empowerment.

> "Blessed are you poor, for yours is the kingdom of God. Blessed are you that hunger now, for you shall be satisfied. Blessed are you that weep now, for you shall laugh."
>
> Luke 6:20–21, RSV

# CHAPTER 8

# Living Out
# the Fullness of the Gospel
# in the
# Peaceable Realm

All through the year after the event described in the previous chapter, I heard many accounts that it had been a life-changing experience. A year later, I revisited the same conference. Many of the planners were participants in the previous conference. One of the Asian American planning committee members who was not at the event a year ago commented to me: "This is the most sensitive group of white people I have ever met." Apparently they were using what they had learned. Again, they gave a lot of attention to including people of color for this event. As a result, there was a very good representation of American Indians and Asian Americans.

During the conference, they decided to use the group division technique again. The participants were divided into three groups: whites, American Indians, and Asian Americans. The task was for each group to work for a period of time, and when they returned, they would share something about their cultures and histories with the whole group.

The Asian Americans gave a report covering some history of each of the Asian groups represented. They mentioned the Japanese internment during World War II, the Chinese Exclusion Act, etc. They also covered many positive aspects of their cultures, such as the support of the extended family structure and their emphasis on education.

The American Indians were much younger. They gave personal accounts of some of the native rituals in which they participated while they were growing up. It evolved into a question-and-answer session where the whites and the Asian Americans asked the questions and the American Indians answered. We all learned a lot.

In stark contrast, the white group's report consisted of one big "I am sorry!" They gave a litany of how whites oppressed all the different groups beginning with the American Indians, then the African Americans, and then the Asians and the Hispanics. At the end of their report, they were depressed, and the Asian Americans and American Indians looked at each other with a look that appeared to say, "What are we supposed to do with that?"

Later that day, there was an opportunity for the previous year's participants to share their experiences. A few people of color actually believed that they had become the oppressors when they claimed their power by asking the whites to be silent and listen. The white group's report earlier in the conference confirmed their uneasy feeling of being the oppressors. At that point, I realized that last year's experience was only the beginning for this group of young people. There needed to be a continuation of the process. The powerful cannot stay powerful, and the powerless cannot stay powerless. There needs to be movement between the two in order for the Gospel to come alive for each group.

This movement has to be cyclical. The white group entered into the Gospel cycle through the cross, by giving up power in the event a year earlier. However, they did not make any movement from there. They stayed powerless. The guilt that came with recognizing their privileges and their ancestors' misuse of their power was so strong that they had become paralyzed. They were not able to distinguish between sharing power and being persecuted. So for the powerful, once they have given up their power, they must continue the cycle to move from death to resurrection. Death without resurrection is a total loss. The cross without the empty tomb is nothing but a symbol of death.

The entry point for the people of color in this situation was through the empowerment of the resurrection. But they could not stay there because they might become too powerful and stand at risk of becoming the oppressors. I did not think in this case that they had become the oppressors. However, since the white group remained powerless a year later, it looked as though they had become the oppressors. In any case, they needed to continue the cycle and learn to share the power that they had just gained. Many reactions to strong ethnic groups and women's groups in the name of "reverse" racism or sexism may be caused by this fear that the powerless will become too powerful. But I believe there needs to be a lot more empowerment of people of color before this fear is justified. If every group that comes into power begins to explore the spirituality of the cross, then the fear of the oppressed becoming the oppressor will be eliminated. The cycle of the cross and the empty tomb must continue. If not, we will be abusing our power.

Figure 8.1 represents the cycle of Gospel living in a multicultural community. Notice that the entry point for whites and people of color are different. Whites enter the cycle by giving up power and bearing the cross. People of color enter the cycle by endurance, faithfulness, empowerment, and resurrection. Once both groups have entered the cycle, they must continue to move around the cycle or they will risk abusing their power and becoming paralyzed by guilt.

**Figure 8.1**
**Cycle of Gospel Living**

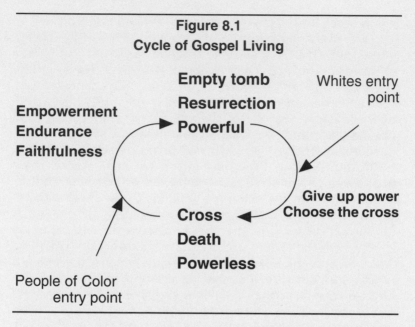

Every Christian is called to live out the cycle of the cross and resurrection, Lent and Easter. In a multicultural society, living out this cycle becomes even more crucial. Leaders are often called to be "Robin Hoods" of power—to take power from the powerful and give it to the powerless. For example, I was a music minister for a conference in which the majority were whites. One of my goals was to present music that was inclusive of the ethnic cultures in the church. After an African-American hymn was introduced, a group of whites complained that the language in the hymn was sexist and demanded that the male references to God (i.e., Lord) be changed. The African Americans did not want to make the change and were on the verge of calling the request racist. The white group was close to calling the African Americans sexists. I did a power analysis of the situation based on the cultural contexts of the group involved. From the context of the African-American history and culture, I drew the conclusion that the predominant use of "Lord" to refer to God was very important to the African American.

Because of their experience of slavery, they responded to the God of the Hebrew scripture—an all-powerful Lord who would deliver them from the hardship of slavery. The need to see God as strong and powerful was crucial to the survival of the African Americans.

I also evaluated the situation from the context of the white liberal American culture. In this context, a cultural assumption was that all people were equal. With the help of the feminist movement, there was the need to see men and women as equal. Furthermore, since humankind, both male and female, is made in the image of God, to continue to image God in exclusively male terms is unacceptable. Therefore, there was the need to change all male references to God to more gender-neutral terms.

I then analyzed the context of this encounter and realized the African Americans were the minority and were perceived by others as powerless. The white group, even though their concern was valid in their own cultural context, were perceived as powerful. Based on this analysis, I decided to continue singing the African American hymns without any changes because, in this situation, it might be more important to support the African Americans. However, I tried to counterbalance this decision by intentionally introducing new hymns with feminine images of God to the whole group. I wanted to affirm the importance of inclusive language but not at the expense of taking power away from a group that was already perceived as powerless. We can see the complexity of doing justice in a multicultural community.

I practice this cycle of Gospel living myself as I exist between two cultures. When I am in a church meeting with a white majority, I become very outspoken sometimes, speaking on behalf of the powerless. When I am with a Chinese community, I know I am respected and given power because of my ordained status. I use my power very carefully. I become very humble and try to find ways to empower others in that community. When I worked in a small Chinese ministry that worshiped in the cathedral of the diocese, I walked through this cycle within the same day, sometimes several times. For example, I would have a meeting with the diocesan committee representing the Chinese ministry—a time to know I was blessed and resurrected and empowered by the Holy Spirit to challenge the system. In the afternoon, I would visit a Chinese church member—a time to serve, be humble, and empower others by taking up the cross. Then, I would have a meeting with the bishop—time to be resurrected again. That evening, I would have a Chinese Bible study group—time to take up the cross again.

There is much fear associated with giving power away. People feel that once they do, they will be powerless forever. But that fear is based on the assumption that people in general like to keep the power that they have. This assumption, which may be true in the world today, is a source of evil. In our fear of becoming powerless, we hold on to whatever power and material goods that we have. As long as we give in to this fear, we are supporting the evil system where there is no justice—no even distribution of power. Jesus combats evil by facing the fear of powerlessness. Jesus lets go of power, dies on the cross, and triumphs over evil. Much of the Gospel teaches us to give power away and not be afraid of becoming powerless, because in our powerlessness we will become powerful in combating the evil of the world.

Imagine a world where all who have power give their power away to those who have less. Those who give their power away to those who have less will become powerless initially. But this does not happen just once. If everyone has the same value, then the people who received power earlier and therefore have become more powerful, will give their power back to those who have become powerless. So the more we give away, the more we receive. Try the following exercise. Say you have ten people in the room. Give two people ten chips each. The instruction is that when you have more chips than others, you give them away until you have none. This could be a lot of fun. You realize after a while that the exercise becomes an endless sequence of giving and receiving. No one is ever left without any chip even though you are instructed to give them all away. The more times you give yours away, the more times you will receive.

This is the dynamic of living the Gospel. This is what the Peaceable Realm is about. This is what the Kingdom of God is like. If everyone learned to give power away, the Kingdom of God would be here. "Your Kingdom come..." in the Lord's Prayer would be realized.

The question then is, "How do you give your power away?" This is one of those things that is more easily said than done. Giving power away is scary. There is the fear of chaos, being out of control, and even being hurt. It takes a very secure person to do that. In the next chapter, I will introduce a process called "Mutual Invitation," which exemplifies how to give power away. The more we practice giving, the more we will be comfortable with it. It becomes like a process of breathing in and out. We cannot breathe out all the time or we suffocate. On the other hand, we cannot breathe in all the time or we hyperventilate. This rhythm of breathing in and out, giving and receiving, becoming powerful and powerless, is the rhythm of living the Gospel fully.

# CHAPTER 9

# Mutual Invitation
## as
## Mutual
## Empowerment

In Chapter Five, we learned the validity of the two kinds of communities in a multicultural environment. One is the monocultural community in which, especially for communities of color, people can function naturally and comfortably within their cultural boundaries. The purpose of monocultural community is twofold: (1) to find identity and self-esteem as a group; and (2) to do homework together before encountering other cultural communities.

The second kind of community consists of a time and place where these different monocultural communities can encounter each other in true dialogue. This requires the leaders of the communities to be intentional about drawing culturally diverse people together. It also requires commitment from all participants because each person will be asked to step beyond his or her cultural boundaries. Most of them will be asked to behave in very unnatural ways. Initially there will be confusion, frustration, and conflict. But the participants need to know that if they work through the initial discomfort, they will be able to experience temporarily a true multicultural community. These communities need to be temporary because it is unrealistic to expect people to function outside their cultural boundaries all the time. Sometimes the anxiety is too great. One friend of mine described her experience in a multicultural environment as walking into a mine field. "You never know when you are triggering a bomb." People need to "go home" to their own comfortable cultural environment. That is where they can process their experience further and use what they have learned.

I have already covered in Chapter Three the different expectations that white and people-of-color communities have of their leaders. In this and the next two chapters, I want to explore what kind of leadership is needed in the second kind of community, the multicultural community. I will be describing processes that I have tested in multicultural groups, and I will be sharing the concepts and theories behind how they work. I call these processes a *spirituality* because these processes, if used regularly, become a discipline of everyday life. Let me begin by exploring the concept of invitation.

As Jesus passed along the Sea of Galilee, he saw Simon and his brother Andrew casting a net into the sea—for they were fishermen. And Jesus said to them, "Follow me and I will make you fish for people." And immediately they left their nets and followed him. As he went a little farther, he saw James son of Zebedee and his brother John, who were in their boat mending the nets. Immediately he called them;

and they left their father Zebedee in the boat with the hired men, and followed him.

Mark 1:16–20

When we need participants in our programs, we usually stand in front of the congregation and ask for volunteers. Imagine Jesus asking for volunteers to become his disciples. He would stand by the seaside and say, "Anyone who is interested in hearing what I have to say, please follow me." Sounds strange, doesn't it? If Jesus asked for volunteers, James, John, Simon, and Andrew would not have followed him because voluntarism assumed that the volunteers already had a strong sense of their individual power. Fishermen in Jesus' time were probably on the lower end of the economic ladder. A fisherman would say, "He couldn't be calling me. He must have meant the well-educated, influential people standing over there." Jesus knew this; so he simply issued a direct invitation and they accepted.

An alternative to volunteering is invitation. Invitation is a way of giving away power. Accepting an invitation is a way to claim power. Waiting to be invited is a way to take up the cross. Invitation becomes a spiritual discipline for multicultural leaders.

Before discussing this topic further, it might be helpful to consider the typical ways we function in groups. Three processes dominate group dynamics. My experience has proved to me that none of these processes works very well in a multicultural setting.

First is the volunteer process. In this process, participants are asked to volunteer information whenever they are ready to share, in no particular order. An assumption of this process is that everyone has a strong sense of his or her individual power and is comfortable speaking out in a group without a direct invitation. If this is used in a multicultural group, as we have seen, most of the time the white members of the group volunteer first. Then there is an unbearable silence while the group is waiting for the people of color to volunteer. This process can be very time consuming. A lot of time is wasted in the anxiety of not knowing what the silence means. The leader might eventually end the process without hearing from everybody by saying something like, "We need to respect people's need to be silent." Whether this "need to be silent" is real for those who do not speak is not relevant. This is usually done in the name of keeping a set schedule and very often for the sake of those who feel guilty that they have not been able to include everybody in the process.

The second typical process is "going around in a circle," in which each participant takes his or her turn to speak. This process, although it includes everybody, creates a great deal of anxiety and is not conducive to listening. If I am sitting next to the person who is sharing and I know I am next, I spend my time thinking about what I am going to say instead of listening to what is being shared. The advantage of this process is that it moves the process along. There is no waiting. In fact, there is very little silence between speakers. As soon as one finishes, the next person jumps right in. Sometimes what is shared may be brief. There is an impression that the speaker cannot wait to finish.

The third typical process is the "commander" method, in which the leader calls on whomever he or she pleases. This is mostly used in a High Power Distance culture and in large American businesses. Many people of color are quite at home with this way of functioning. Many actually need a direct invitation to speak because they need to know that they are designated as the person with authority to speak. Whites dislike this process even though they tolerate it in the hierarchical structures of corporate or church environments. Sometimes they accuse the leader of being dictatorial. This process gives too much power to one person. If the leader is sensitive to the needs of the group, this process can be very effective and efficient. However, if the leader is interested only in his or her own agenda, he or she will just call on whomever will support the leader's view. Because of the power this person has, no one will challenge what is going on.

A process I have created that works very well with multicultural groups is called "Mutual Invitation." This is how it goes. I, as the leader, first share without projecting myself as an expert. After I have spoken, I then invite someone to share. I usually do not invite the person next to me because that might set up the precedent of going around in a circle. After the next person has spoken, that person is given the privilege of inviting another to share. The person being invited has the option to "pass" if she does not want to say anything. After a person says "pass," he is still given the privilege to invite another to share. This continues until everybody has had a chance to share.

This process might seem very simple and insignificant, but the ramifications of it are quite incredible, even to me. I started introducing this process two years ago as an experiment in many groups that I worked with. About a year after the initial introduction of this process, I started receiving calls from people asking where this process originated. When I said I created it, they reported how this process had transformed their group's working style.

I was doing a follow-up training for a congregational development team in an Episcopal diocese. The group was organized by the executive officer of the diocese. I had introduced Mutual Invitation to the group six months earlier. At the end of a meeting that I was to observe and provide feedback, the executive officer invited a member of the group to lead the next meeting. This woman accepted the invitation and then immediately invited another person to offer an opening worship for the next meeting. The person accepted the invitation with a smile. During the break, the executive officer came to me with a sparkle in his eyes and said, "It's simple. One, two, three and it's done. Did you see that? This invitation thing is incredible. Before you came six months ago, I would ask for volunteers, and they would look at each other. That was painful. Now, I invite and it is done. The next time, she would invite the next meeting chair. Everybody knows that they would have their turns. I don't have to be in charge all the time. What a relief!"

This process of mutual invitation decentralizes the power that is usually held by the designated leader. In this process, the facilitator spends some time introducing the process, shares, and invites the next person. At that point, the facilitator ceases to have power to control because who will speak next is now up to the person to whom he or she has just given the power to speak. This is what giving power away means. It is a practical way of practicing the spirituality of the cross. To many whites who are used to being in control, this process can be very uncomfortable. To some, it is a relief because anxiety and stress tend to come with having power all the time.

To whites, waiting to be invited is another way of practicing the spirituality of the cross. I was facilitating a diocesan staff development retreat. I described Mutual Invitation as an introduction process. After I modeled by introducing myself to the group, the bishop asked, "Can I go next?" I said, "No, bishop." You could hear the gasps in the room.

"According to the process I just described," I continued, "I now have the power to invite the next person to share and I choose to invite someone else. Your turn will come up. I am sorry for this but I think by trusting the process there is something to be learned. So please bear with me on this."

The bishop complied. He was invited to speak immediately after the next person had spoken. For the rest of the day, he respected the process. At a few rounds, he was the last person invited. The bishop, situated on top of the church hierarchy, had to wait to be invited by a support staff before he spoke. This was humility. This was an exercise of the miracle of the ear.

In this Mutual Invitation process, the lions and the wolves and the bears are asked to refrain from using their power freely. They are asked to wait for their turn. They are asked to listen to others and not worry about controlling and directing the movement of the group. They are asked to exercise humility, take up the cross, and exercise the miracle of the ear again and again. Yet, they are also given their share of time and space to exercise power so that they can maintain their sense of power. The consistent practice of this enables them to become more and more sensitive to others who might not have as strong a sense of power. This helps them appreciate others not based on their ability to stand up to them but on what they have to share and contribute to the group.

This process also manages the silence that usually comes with the volunteer method. Silence in different cultures means different things. For some, silence is a reflective time. For others, it is anxiety-producing, and for still others it communicates disagreement. Whites tend to be very uncomfortable with silence and want to fill it with something. For many people of color, silence communicates a wide range of emotion and information that only a person from the same cultural background can read. In a multicultural group, when someone is silent, how does the rest of the group interpret it? Does this person have something to say but is too shy? Does this person not care about what is going on in the group? Is the person offended and silently protesting? Or maybe this person has nothing to say. The anxiety comes from not knowing what the silence means.

This is taken care of by the ground rule: say "pass" if you don't want to say anything. With this ground rule, once an invitation is issued, the person invited to speak is given the time, space, and power to express herself. The person can choose to be in silence first to put her thoughts together before speaking. The person is also given the responsibility to let the whole group know whether she is ready to speak by having the option to pass. In other words, if the person is silent, and he has not said pass, that means the silence is a useful and meaningful time for the person and should be respected. Here, there is no need to interpret silence. The group already knows that the silence is meaningful to the person who has the power at the moment.

I trained a young adult named Keith to conduct Community Bible Study (see Appendix C), which used Mutual Invitation as the principal way for the group to share insights about the Scriptures. Keith's group had two Japanese teenagers who passed every time they were invited to share. My guess was that because they were the youngest in the group, they did not feel they had the power to speak as equals in the group. After four sessions, they still had not said anything. Keith came to me and asked, "Am I doing something wrong? Should I talk to them after the session and ask them why?"

"Were they given the privilege to invite after they passed?" I asked.

"Yes."

"Did the rest of the group keep inviting them even though they passed each time?"

"Yes."

"Then you have to trust the process. Keep doing it for two more sessions and if they still don't talk, we'll work on it together to find another way."

Keith went back and facilitated the group again without any procedural change. The two teenagers passed again. But after the session, they asked Keith for the scriptural passage that they would study next week. Keith gave it to them. Next week, as soon as they were invited to speak, they were ready and spoke with abundance.

When a person says "pass," that person is still given the privilege to invite. We give the message that even if you don't say anything, you are still valued as a full member of the group. The one who passes does not need to justify why he does not want to say anything. This stops people from rescuing others who have a weaker sense of their own power. In a volunteer method, some people would push and coerce the less verbal members to speak. It usually sounds like this: "Come on. You can talk. There is no need to be afraid. We really like to hear what you have to say." This kind of action is patronizing. By accepting a pass without explanation, we respect that the person is able to take care of herself. Expecting people to take care of themselves is one way of empowerment.

In the case of the two teenagers, they took care of themselves by doing extra preparation, knowing that they would be invited again. If Keith had rescued them by trying hard to get them to talk, it might reinforce their feeling of inadequacy. They might even withdraw further. By leaving them alone and not asking for an explanation, the group was giving the message that they trusted them to be able to take care of themselves. In a volunteer method, people who do not speak very much will eventually be ignored as useless to the group. By persistent invitation, we are letting the powerless know that the window of opportunity is always there for them when they are ready to accept and exercise their power.

When I first introduced the process, I discovered that people with a weaker sense of their power sometimes forget to invite the next person to share. I had to remind them that they had that privilege. So many people, especially young people of color, are never given any power. The idea that they had the power to decide who would speak next is very foreign to them. I was conducting a conference for young adults in Miami, Florida. Everyone in this group was a person of color. The first round of Mutual Invitation was slow and uncomfortable because almost everyone forgot to invite after passing or sharing. I did not give in and invite the next speaker on their behalf. I simply reminded them that they still had that power to invite. We did Mutual Invitation for every segment of interaction all day. By the end of the day, the group was actually enjoying the privilege to invite. From the body language and tone of voice they used, I could tell that this group's self-esteem had increased tremendously. Next morning, I did not specify that the group should use Mutual Invitation. Some volunteered to speak; others were silent. Then, one of the shyest women in the group said to another participant, "I haven't heard from you. I invite you to share." That was empowerment at work.

Mutual Invitation gives everyone the experience to exercise power. It also offers the opportunity to use power again and again. The repeated experience of power enables powerless people eventually to claim their share of power with ease and comfort. Sometimes a lamb needs to be told again and again that he or she is not weak but is as strong as the lions and the wolves in the Peaceable Realm. The lamb may not believe it at first, but if the invitation to exercise power is persistently there, the lamb may eventually believe it.

Mutual Invitation is by no means perfect. For example, during each round there is always someone who comes last. This may create some anxiety for that person. I am excited about this simple process because, imperfect as it may be, it does work better than the "traditional" ways of doing things. I am sure there are other methods that work just as well, if not better. The response to this process has been so overwhelming that I would encourage the reader to practice this process for a period of time and see if there is any change in your organization or group. One unique thing about this process is that it has a life of its own. It does not rely on the level of cultural sensitivity of the leader or facilitator to make it work. In every case, once the leader gives instructions on how Mutual Invitation works, the process takes over. This is what I called a form-centered gathering. In Chapter Eleven, we will explore this concept of leadership in depth.

# CHAPTER 10

# *Media as Means of Distributing Power*

We declare to you what was from the beginning, what we have heard, what we have seen
with our eyes, what we have looked at and
touched with our hands, concerning the word
of life—this life was revealed, and we have seen
it and testify to it, and declare to you the eternal
life that was with the Father and was revealed
to us—we declare to you what we have seen
and heard so that you also may have fellowship
with us; and truly our fellowship is with the
Father and with his Son Jesus Christ. We are
writing these things so that our joy may be
complete.

1 John 1:1–4

John clearly stated that the Gospel was not just words on a
page. Contrary to how we in the twentieth century receive
the Gospel (as written words), John emphasized what he
heard, saw, and touched as testimonies. Writing it down was
only a part of the whole process "so that our joy may be
complete." In order for the Gospel to come to life and
empower our communities, we must enable people to see,
hear, and touch it. However, most church leaders use verbal

communication exclusively to conduct church affairs: Bible studies, meetings, group discussions, etc. Verbal communication alone is a biased means of communication, favoring people who have a strong sense of individual power and verbal ability—the majority of whom are whites. Verbal ability is often confused with good leadership. It constitutes only a small part of how human beings communicate. Furthermore, the degree of comfort in using verbal communication varies from culture to culture. Some cultures, especially ones that emphasize the collective over the individual, tend to use fewer words to communicate. People from these cultures assume a lot because of the long tradition of living as collectives rather than as individuals. Therefore, much communication is done nonverbally. Silence is used a lot to communicate a variety of feelings and information. One cannot ignore the visual media of facial expressions and the body language when communicating with people in these cultures.

On the other hand, cultures that favor the individual over the collective tend to use an abundance of words to communicate with each other. Since people in these cultures have been living as individuals and the living units are much smaller, they make fewer assumptions about each other. Therefore, they feel the need to explain everything to make sure the other understands. People from these cultures are quite comfortable in communicating verbally. Silence is often interpreted as consent, apathy, or inability to communicate.[1]

In a society in which verbal ability is favored as good leadership, this cultural difference in the style of communication compounds even further the power dynamics in a multicultural group. Inevitably those from a less verbal culture feel inferior to those from a more verbal culture. Their silence is always interrupted and misunderstood. In order to

---

[1]For an extensive discussion on differences in communication styles, see Edward T. Hall, *Beyond Culture* (New York, London, Toronto, Sydney, Auckland: Doubleday, 1976), p. 91. Hall pioneered the use of the terms "high and low context cultures" to describe the key cultural difference.

enable people of a multicultural community to communicate with each other, we must move beyond using verbal communication exclusively. We must explore the other senses in order to make communication more holistic in a multicultural community. We must learn to provide media by which people can see, hear, and touch each other when they communicate.

Our generation grew up with media—print, visual, audio—which constitutes a major part of what we see, hear, and even touch every day. In order for us to address the issue of justice, which has to do with distribution of power, we cannot ignore the power of media in our world today. Mass media serves to let people from different cultures and nations see and hear how each other lives and what each other's values are. Therefore, a discussion on media can be very fruitful as we move further toward finding concrete ways to realize the Peaceable Realm.

Media, both print and electronic, have always been associated with power distribution. For example, before the movable-type printing press was invented, power resided with the few individuals who had the wisdom of old age. In the church, power resided with the persons who owned a particular copy of the Bible or who could memorize scriptures in maintaining the oral tradition of the church. Media in the church consisted of painters, sculptors, and scribes. In fact, the artists and the scribes were the theologians who communicated the faith through handwriting and painting, sculpture and music. After printing was invented, printed materials, particularly the Bible, were distributed to many more people. Therefore power was decentralized. The invention of printing created an obsession with the print media that has lasted to the present in the Western world. To acquire power meant getting an education through books. A college degree conferred power because it implied that one had read a large number of books.

With the invention of electronics, acquiring power also means owning more electronic media. The more electronic gadgets you own, the more power you have. A person who has a telephone has the power to talk to another person halfway around the world, whereas a person who has no telephone is limited by the distance between her and the person with whom she wants to speak. A person who has a computer can have much more memory and computation power than a person who has only a calculator, who in turn has more power than one who does not have either. A person who has a television can see and hear much more of the world than one who doesn't own one.

Empowerment in the twentieth century involves working with all three kinds of power acquisition: (1) acquiring knowledge and learning to express oneself through visual media and oral tradition, (2) learning to read and write so one can use and create print media, and (3) gaining access to electronic media.

A skilled multicultural group leader must learn how to use media in a way where power can be evenly distributed. We simply cannot run away from using media if we are to work for justice today. There are different kinds of media. The most popular one is the mass media—newspapers, magazines, television, and radio—which is one-way communication with very limited immediate feedback from the audience and readers. For our purpose, I want to focus on a lesser known type of media called group media. Group media includes those forms that enhance interpersonal communication in a group, as opposed to mass media, which is one-way communication to a mass audience. Group media is two-way communication. It is the use of a particular medium to help individuals to express themselves, and it is also the use of a particular medium to help individuals to listen and understand each other. By introducing group media to a group, a leader not only helps individuals to express themselves better, but also has an effective means to address the power dynamics that are set up in multicultural groups. Group media also serves to lower the anxiety level of the participants and, if used effectively, helps to distribute power among group members. A group medium can be photographs, slides, posters, music, audio and videotapes, drawings, drama, writings, etc.

Let me use an example of a simple process to illustrate this. In a situation in which a leader needs to elicit information from a group, the usual way is simply to ask people to volunteer the information—let those who have something to say, say it. In a multicultural group, this does not work, especially when the information you want is personal. The group medium I use is writing on a piece of paper. I invite members of the group to write the information down on a piece of paper. These pieces of paper are then collected and read anonymously by someone who does not recognize the handwriting of the participants. These responses are then recorded on a large piece of paper on the wall so that all can see it. This process ensures all an opportunity to share their thoughts and it lowers the anxiety level of those who normally would not be comfortable speaking as an individual in a group.

This medium also allows more than one thing to happen at a time. Verbal communication is linear—one word after another, one sentence at a time, and one person speaking at a time. In the linear process, many valuable thoughts and ideas can be lost because information does not follow the linear logic of what is being said by other participants. When we add this medium to the process, the participants express themselves on the pieces of paper all at the same time without the influence of others. The information collected is therefore multidimensional and represents the diversity of the group more fully. This medium, limited as it may be, includes everyone.

The second group medium of the process is recording the information on a large piece of paper. This medium gives the group a sense of a community voice—the "we"— even though people do not know which individual provides what information. This is the most basic way to use media: to redistribute power. We are basically inviting each person to be the painter, sculptor, or scribe to communicate his or her ideas and feelings. Once the information, the ideas, and the feelings are written down, recorded on tape, or painted on a piece of paper, they become tangible. You can see them, and you can touch them.

Another example of group media that I use a lot is Photolanguage,[2] which consists of 48 to 96 photographs. I display the photographs on tables so that participants can move around the tables and see them. I then invite each participant to pick one or two photographs that express his or her feelings and ideas on a particular topic. When the participants return with their photographs, each person is given time to share and explain his or her photographs. (For a detailed description of the process, see Appendix B.)

This group medium again provides room for everyone to share. Since all participants have photographs in their hands, all are expected and given the opportunity to express themselves in the group, independent of perception of power and verbal ability. Also, photographs provide a more concrete way for people to express themselves. A word may cause people to see different understandings and images. An image is concrete, and when a person is using an

---

[2]About twenty years ago, a team of Roman Catholic catechists and educators in France began to explore ways to use photographs in youth groups. Their goals were (1) to search for a language close to the daily life experience of youth, and (2) to find a method by which to study in depth the problems common to a group. At that time, reports of Paulo Freire's work with the farmers in Brazil were being circulated in Europe. Freire also used photos to help farmers communicate their experiences, which led to concrete actions. Based on these parallel movements, the team of educators and catechists in France created "Photolanguage" as a tool and method for group work that elicits verbal expression, allows a more holistic and personal approach to problems, provokes affective response, stimulates imagination, and helps focus on the task at hand. They were first used in the catechetical context of the Roman Catholic Church. However, later development and research led to the use of this tool for adults, premarital group work, and the elderly. In 1980, I studied the use of Photolanguage in France with the originators, particularly Alain Baptiste and Pierre Babin. I returned to the United States and began developing a set of Photolanguage for use locally. As a result of eight years of testing, I had published the first set of forty-eight photos entitled "INTERACTIONS." I took the original concept and process and modified them to create new ways to use Photolanguage for multicultural groups. I believe that Photolanguage is one of the most effective ways to enhance multicultural group communication.

image to describe what he or she wants to say, there is less of a chance for that person to be misinterpreted. Also, an image enables people to communicate symbolically. The intuition, feeling, and creativity that an image conjures up in people provide channels for the group members to communicate with each other in greater depth. It would take much more time for verbal communication alone to accomplish such depth in communication because verbal communication is linear and one dimensional. Images are at least two-dimensional, and they provide additional perspectives that give a more complete and whole picture of what is being communicated. Drawing a picture and creating a sculpture are group media that have a similar effect.

If a group uses this kind of visual group media regularly, the group will accumulate a common symbol system that does not rely on their own cultural assumptions. For example, I was conducting a retreat on the theme of racism. I used Photolanguage to help participants explore the definition and effect of racism on their lives. In this process, a few people picked a photo of keys. One participant explained, "Racism has to do with who has the key to open which door. As a person of color, the keys I have are limited. I don't have the ones to open the doors that I want, such as education and financial security."

"Not only that," another participant added, "sometimes they give you a key but it doesn't open any door. So you end up frustrated because you have only the dream and you can't get there."

Another participant commented on how the keys are chained together in different rings. She said, "The people who have the keys also band together to protect what they have. They are the people who profit from racism. They have the power to maintain the system that allows them to continue to profit from it and they are not going to give anyone their keys unless you also support that system."

Throughout the rest of the retreat, the image of the keys surfaced again and again as a common symbol for the group to describe racism. By using the medium of photographs, this group created a vocabulary that they shared. It

was almost like a new language in which everyone had a common assumption and understanding of each word. In a multicultural setting, people from different cultures bring with them cultural assumptions, beliefs, and values that are very different from one person to another. These differences, when expressed only through words, are often the sources of conflict because there is no common understanding behind the words being used. Developing a common symbol system is essential for a successful intercultural encounter. Without it, the group wastes a lot of time trying to define terms and clear up misunderstandings. Visual group media can help a group to develop such a common symbol system. With the advances of electronic media today, the use of media is unlimited. Here are a few possibilities:

1. Give each person or group a tape recorder. Invite them to record their answer to a question. Then, as a total group, have everyone listen to all the tapes and then discuss.

2. Give each person or group a camera and teach them how to use it. Invite them to take pictures that represent the problems in society. Develop the pictures. Put the photograph on the wall and use them to discuss the problems.

3. Give each group a video camera and teach them how to use it. Invite them to record interactions that they see as important in their communities. Replay all tapes and discuss.

Leadership in a multicultural community requires direct invitation to engage in dialogue. Once people are there, a leader must continue the invitation to participate but also provide holistic channels for people to communicate. Verbal communication alone is not sufficient because it favors the white members of the group. A leader must learn to use group media as ways to include everyone and to help people express themselves more fully. Through group media, a group can also develop a common symbol system by which they can understand each other without the clouding of different cultural assumptions. Finally, a leader must facilitate the group to use different media to express themselves so that others can hear, see, and touch what they are trying to communicate.

> We declare to you what was from the beginning, what we have heard, what we have seen with our eyes, what we have looked at and touched with our hands, concerning the word of life.
>
> 1 John 1:1

# CHAPTER 11

# *Liturgy as Spiritual Discipline for Leadership in a Multicultural Community*

They shall not hurt or destroy in all my holy
mountain;
for the earth shall be full of the
knowledge of the LORD
as the waters cover the sea.
                          Isaiah 11:9, RSV

My denomination, the Episcopal Church, spends a lot of time on the liturgy—the forms and rituals of public, corporate worship. We spent convention after convention debating the revision of liturgy in the '70s. Episcopal Church leaders spend countless hours preparing for the Sunday liturgy every week. Which song to sing? Which "prayer of the people" to use? Who will read the Scripture lessons? Who will lead the prayers? What color banner should be displayed? What theme to preach? On Sunday, it all comes together. The sacraments of the church *are* realized, and, hopefully, the presence of God is recognized and revealed to all who participate.

Liturgy is a prescribed format of words and interactions that create a sacred time and space in which the people of God may experience the holy. It is amazing and puzzling to me to see churches, which spend so much time in preparing their liturgies, spend so little time preparing for meetings, especially meetings involving more than one cultural group. We devote so much time making sure the Spirit may flow during the liturgy, but when it comes to a meeting, we do nothing, as if we rely solely on the Spirit to do her job alone. A sense of co-creation is lost somehow. We leave the interaction and the form of the meeting up to the person in charge. Depending on this person's cultural and professional background, the meeting proceeds with or without intentional input from our faith and our knowledge of liturgy.

For example, I have seen many group ministries grow and flourish for a year and then disappear. When I ask the people why, they say that their leader, who was "wonderful," had left to do something else and then the ministry fell apart. Leadership in the church outside the liturgy lies heavily with the leader. Since we have this person-centered bias in church leadership, we spend hour after hour, conference after conference, training persons to take leadership in the church. Since these training programs depend on the trainer's skill and knowledge, the level of skills acquired vary from person to person. As a result, the fate of the many churches' group ministries becomes a roller coaster ride of ups and downs depending on the person in the leadership position.

In a multicultural situation, this person-centered leadership style is even more problematic. Depending on his or her cultural background, the leader could function in a volunteer style or a directive style. If this person does not have intercultural awareness training, staying with these styles of group interaction will most likely exclude some people or the leader will be challenged by others in the group. Intercultural sensitivity takes time and training. We cannot assume that all our leaders are interculturally sensitive, nor can we ensure that every leader is trained to be interculturally sensitive. The concept of liturgy may provide a solution to this problem.

In a liturgy, all the leaders work with the prescribed forms that govern the interaction of the gathering. A liturgy has essential components, and each component is protected by the community's affirmation of such a form. For example, the Holy Eucharist in the Episcopal Church must have the following components: gather in the Lord's name, proclaim and respond to the Word of God, pray for the world and the church, exchange the peace, prepare the table, make eucharist, break the bread, share the gifts of God, and dismiss the people. In that sense, the liturgy itself is the leader. A liturgy centers around a form. If a priest strays from this form too far, the whole congregation would know and take action to correct it. Even though the priest still has a lot of power to control how the liturgy should proceed, he or she cannot abuse that power because of the public knowledge of the form. If the form is understood and affirmed by everyone in the community, there is a corporate sense of making sure that the liturgy is done right so that the presence of God is known through it.

Another advantage of having a liturgy is that it reduces the amount of training time for someone to participate in leadership positions. For example, it would take a lot of time to teach someone how to conduct a public prayers section of the worship. With a liturgy, you need only to have a copy of the written form of the prayer of the people and simply invite the person to read it. The only training needed is how to read aloud in public worship. Also, to lead a liturgy one does not have to understand everything that is in it. There is a sense of mystery. Liturgy does not talk about what each word and interaction means but simply immerses participants in the form. Through this immersion, participants gain a fuller knowledge of God "as the waters cover the sea."

We must shift the church's leadership style from person-centered to form-centered—that is, transform the skills needed to manage a multicultural group into liturgies. These liturgies would enable people from different cultural backgrounds to coexist side by side without hurting each other. These liturgies would create a holy mountain on which the Peaceable Realm can be realized. If such liturgies exist, then the only training needed for our church leaders is the implementation of the liturgies.

The Mutual Invitation process described in Chapter Nine is one such liturgy. In the "holy" space and time set up by this process, each person has power to communicate and is respected and listened to. A leader may not understand how this process empowers some people and humbles others. As long as the leader values the process—this liturgy—true communication and mutual empowerment will happen. This happens just as a liturgical leader might not understand the mystery of how the bread and wine in the eucharist become the body and blood of Jesus Christ. By following the prescribed action and words, it happens. I once asked Walter Wink, the author of *Transforming Bible Study*, how his method of Bible study worked. He said that many theories could be used to describe the working of this process. Even so, he did not understand it completely. But he did know that whenever he did it in the same way, the process somehow transformed people's lives.

What would a liturgy for a multicultural gathering look like? This is a key question that I reflect upon every time I design a workshop or a conference for an intercultural encounter. I want to share with you some of the insights I have gained from my work in search of such a liturgy. The following elements have to be included in the process of the gathering:

1. A clear description of the purpose of the gathering.

2. Clearly stated ground rules of interaction affirmed by everyone in the gathering.

3. Clear procedural instructions before each segment of interaction.

4. A segment of time for building interpersonal relationships.

5. A segment of time for working together on tasks.

6. Reflection on the experience and the recording of important learning.

7. Discussion of how to apply the learning to future gatherings.

This process implies very careful planing before each gathering. It also implies that the process will continue to evolve because the learning you gain from doing it will help you redesign the next gathering. Here is an example of what a liturgy for an intercultural dialogue group looks like.

## I. Opening Prayers and Purpose of Gathering

*The leader may read the following opening prayer or some other suitable prayer.*

Let us begin our meeting with a prayer. Let us pray:

O God, you made us in your own image and redeemed us through Jesus your Son: Look with compassion on the whole human family; take away the arrogance and hatred that infect our hearts; break down the walls that separate us; unite us in bonds of love; and work through our struggle and confusion to accomplish your purposes on earth; that, in your good time, all nations and races may serve you in harmony around your heavenly throne; through Jesus Christ our Lord. Amen.

*The leader continues by reading the following purpose statement of the gathering.*

The purpose of this gathering is to bring together people from diverse ethnic and cultural backgrounds to engage in dialogue with each other. True dialogue is a conversation on a common subject between two or more persons of differing views. The primary purpose of dialogue is for each person to learn from the other so that he or she can change and grow.[1] We believe our commitment to dialogue with each other will effect constructive change in race relations within the church and in the communities in which we reside.

In the next two hours, we will introduce ourselves to each other, share some childhood experiences, and begin to look at the values that we have.

## II. Communication Guidelines[2] (Ground rules)

*Hand out copies of "Communication Guidelines" (see below). The leader gives the following explanation:*

We, people from different cultural backgrounds, bring with us different assumptions of communication styles. Sometimes, these different assumptions can cause misunderstanding among the participants. Therefore, before we begin our dialogue, we must first state a common communication guideline that we all can agree upon.

*The leader or a designated person will read the Communication Guidelines.*

1. We are not here to debate who is right and who is wrong. We are here to experience true dialogue in which we strive to communicate honestly and listen actively and openly to each other. (For religious groups, dialogue is never an opportunity for proselytizing.) We invite you to open your hearts and minds to experience new ideas, feelings, situations and people even though, at times, the process may be uncomfortable.

---

[1] This definition of dialogue comes from the guidelines for dialogue of the Los Angeles Chapter of the National Conference of Christians and Jews (NCCJ). According to their source, this definition is adapted from Leonard Swindler's article "Dialogue Decalogue."

[2] This set of Communication Guidelines is based on an approach developed by the staff, particularly Lucky Altman, of the Los Angeles Chapter of the NCCJ for use in their dialogue process.

2. Our leaders are not experts. Their role is to provide a structure and process by which we can better communicate with each other.

3. We recognize that we might have preconceived assumptions and perceptions about others. Some are conscious; some are unconscious. We invite you to be aware of how they influence the way you listen and interpret others' words and actions. We also invite you to be aware of how these assumptions affect the way you speak and act in the group. In doing so, we can better maintain our respect for and acceptance of self and others as valuable human beings.

4. We invite you to take responsibility for what you say and what you say on behalf of a group. We also invite you to speak with words that others can hear and understand and, whenever possible, use specific personal examples that relate to the topic being discussed.

5. We invite you to expand your listening sense to include not just words but also feelings being expressed, nonverbal communication such as body language and different ways of using silence.

6. We invite you to take responsibility for your own feelings as they surface. Feelings may be triggered by particular words or actions but they may or may not be directly related to the particular interaction. When that happens, simply communicate that feeling without blaming others. In doing so, members of the group can hear and learn constructively the consequences of our words and actions.

7. We invite you to hold the personal information shared here in confidence because only in this way can we feel free to say what is in our minds and hearts.

*After reading, the leader may ask participants if there are questions and discuss the Guidelines briefly.*

## III. Describe the Mutual Invitation Process

In order to ensure that everyone who wants to share *has* the opportunity to speak, we will proceed in the following way:

The leader or a designated person will share first. After that person has spoken, he or she then invites another to share. Whom you invite does not need to be the person next to you. After the next person has spoken, that person is given the privilege to invite another to share. If you don't want to say anything, simply say "pass" and proceed to invite another to share. We will do this until everyone has been invited. During this gathering we will use this method of sharing at least three times. After that, we can open the floor for general discussion. Is there any question about the process?

*If this is the first time this group uses Mutual Invitation, the leader might want to demonstrate how it may work.*


## IV. Dialogue

*The leader will introduce the first topic of sharing.*

I now invite you to share on the following topic, using the Mutual Invitation process:

Give your name.

What are your hopes for this dialogue?

What brings you to this dialogue group?

*The leader models by sharing first and then starting the Mutual Invitation process. After the first round, the leader introduces the next topic and process.*

Consider a time in your childhood when you realized you were "different." The difference might be your gender, race, class, religion, language, etc. I invite you to spend ten minutes drawing a picture depicting this memory. You may want to represent this memory literally or symbolically. We are not looking for artistic ability here but insights and honesty. Please do this in silence.

*After participants complete the picture, the leader gives the following instructions:*

Continuing with the Mutual Invitation process, I now invite you to share your picture. If you wish, before you share your picture you may spend some time describing where you grew up and how your family spent time together. The person who shared last in the last round may invite a person to start.

*After everyone has shared, the leader invites participants to take a ten-minute break. When everyone returns, the leader introduces the third topic.*

The next topic I invite you to share is: What is one value that I learned from my parents that I would like to pass on to the next generation? Again, the last person who shared may invite the next person.

*After everyone has shared, the leader opens the floor for discussion.*

Are there clarifications that you want to ask each other? Does anyone want to add anything to what they have said?

## V. Reflection on the Experience

*The leader helps the group to reflect on the experience by asking the following questions:*

How did you feel about today's session?

What did you learn?

How can we as a group improve our communication with each other?

*The leader writes down learning and future improvements on newsprint.*

## VI. Closing Prayer

*The leader closes the meeting by saying the following:*

I thank all of you for sharing. I hope that you will come back for our next meeting. To close our time together, I invite you spend a moment to complete the following sentences:

I thank God today...

I ask God today...

*Allow a period of silence. The leader continues.*

Let's join hands in a circle. I will start by sharing, "I thank God today, and I ask God today...." After I am done, I will squeeze the hand of the person on my right. That will be the signal for him/her to offer his/her prayers. When she finishes, she then squeezes the hand of the person on her right. If you don't want to say anything, just pass the pulse to the next person. When the pulse comes back to me, I will start saying the Lord's Prayer and I invite you to join me.

\* \* \*

This is a two-hour liturgy for a first-time intercultural encounter group. Notice the detail of the script. It is just like a liturgy that one would follow in a worship service. It requires the leader only to know how to read clearly and have some basic group skills. Let me go through this process step-by-step to explain why each step is necessary.

## (1) A clear description of the purpose of the gathering.

In multicultural groups, people come to a gathering with very different expectations. For example, one person might expect to make decisions that could effect immediate change. Another might expect simply to make some new friends.

And another might expect to tell the others what the problems are. In order to avoid a misunderstanding, it is crucial to state clearly the purpose of the gathering and define any terms that may have different cultural interpretations. In this case, the opening prayer helps put the gathering in the context of our faith, and the purpose of the gathering and the term *dialogue* are explained.

### (2) Clearly stated ground rules of interaction affirmed by everyone in the gathering.

This step is accomplished by the section on Communication Guidelines. People from different cultural backgrounds will bring with them assumptions of communication styles. Ground rules invite participants to leave their assumptions behind and affirm a common set of guidelines for behavior and attitudes. In other words, in multicultural settings ground rules serve to develop a temporary culture that is shared by the group at the moment.

This communication guideline serves to remind participants that communication is more than just verbal interchange. It involves the whole person: attitudes, speaking, listening, body language, interpreting, etc. It also reminds the participants that there are differences in communication styles among people with different cultural backgrounds. Even though participants may not know what all this means, it is important to communicate it and, at an opportune time, refer back to it. A good time to do this is during the "Reflection" segment. Ground rules are important also to pull the group back to a working state if participants exhibit unacceptable behaviors. It may seem tedious to read all of this material so early in the gathering, but experience shows me that if I don't do it in such detail, people will forget and the time it takes to bring the group back will be much longer than the time spent earlier in the process.

### (3) Clear procedural instructions before each segment of interaction.

Clear instructions help the participants to know what to expect. The level of anxiety decreases as you let the participants know more of what is to come. With Mutual Invitation, the participants know from the beginning that they will have their fair share of time to say what they have to say. Clear instruction here eliminates the anxiety of deciding when to speak up. Clear instruction also helps participants to help each other to proceed. Very often, people who have an unsure sense of personal power forget to invite the next person. With clearly described instructions, group members usually will remind each other to take the privilege of inviting seriously.

## *(4) and (5) A segment of time for building interpersonal relationships and a segment of time for working together on tasks.*

Since the task of this session is to build relationships and understanding, the three rounds of Mutual Invitation take care of both of these segments. At a later dialogue session, the "task" segment may include a session on planning a program for the church and the community or some other concrete task. The use of a group medium, such as drawing a picture, provides an alternative to verbal communication and gives participants another channel to express themselves. The break after the second round of sharing is very important. Up to that point, they have been sharing in a very formal way by inviting each other. The break provides an informal time for people to get to know each other and share some insights.

## *(6) and (7) Reflection on the experience, the recording of important learning, and discussion of how to apply learning to future gatherings.*

Incorporating reflection time is essential if the group is to grow together. Capturing the learning in both content and process helps participants remember and incorporate their learning in their lives and ministries. Here is where the lions realize that they are lions and the lambs find out that they are lambs. Here is where they can learn concrete ways to continue to realize the Peaceable Realm. If there is something good, talk about how you can recreate it and make it better. If something did not go as well, talk about how you can change it next time to correct the problem.

* * *

Once you have a liturgy that works, you can keep the same structure and change the content. In this case, the three topics of discussion can be replaced with new questions and topics in the next session of dialogue. One can also replace the second round with other group media such as Photolanguage, posters on the wall, meditation with a song, a written reflection form, etc. The rest can more or less stay the same.

Experienced group leaders will resist using a script. It may feel wooden and without life. My advice is to start with following the script as closely as possible. This will give you the feel of how this particular process works. Also, it will show the other, less experienced participants that they can be a leader too. Following a script that works and consistently doing it the same way is an empowerment process. Eventually, when you are ready to move on to do something else, it is easy to find a replacement. Anyone in the group will be able to do it because the person is not the leader—the liturgy, the form, is.

I have included in the appendix the "Community Bible Study," which is a well-tested multicultural process. It is a liturgy written for Bible study. I have tested it for more than three years with many different groups. The requirement to lead such a group is to be able read and do no more than one hour of research for a five-minute presentation. You will also find in the appendix detailed descriptions of the "Mutual Invitation" process and "Using Photolanguage in Small Group Communication." These are well-tested liturgies for multicultural groups' work.

A major part of spirituality is discipline. In the Christian monastic community, the discipline of moving through the day with daily offices and communion is the backbone of their spirituality. These liturgies, as prescribed by the community, shape, reshape, and inform members of the community in both explicit and implicit ways. I was working on this book in a monastery. On the first day, I was quite annoyed by the interruption of the bell calling everyone to attend the daily office five times a day. Every time, I had to drop what I was writing, move into a worship space, and shift my mind to a liturgical mode. However, by the second day, I realized that these breaks from my writing were actually good for me because every time I returned from chapel, I got fresh and new insights for my book. The daily prescribed services forced me to behave and think differently from my intellectual routine when I was writing. These intentional changes helped me to see my routine in a new light. In a multicultural community, this kind of discipline is even more crucial. The discipline of practicing the "liturgies" for multicultural gatherings can cause us to break from the routine of our unreflective cultural pattern. In the process, we can see ourselves and our cultural patterns and values more clearly, and we can become more sensitive to different cultures and more skilled in realizing the Peaceable Realm.

# Appendix A

# *Mutual Invitation*

| | |
|---|---|
| *Objectives:* | To facilitate sharing and discussion in a multicultural group. |
| *Type of Group:* | Any. |
| *Size of Group:* | 4–15. |
| *Setting:* | Participants should sit in a circle. |
| *Materials:* | Newsprint and markers. |
| *Time Required:* | Depending on the size of the group. A good way to tell how much time will be required for each round of sharing is to multiply the number of participants by five minutes. |

## *How to Proceed:*

A. *Let participants know how much time is set aside for this process.*

B. *Introduce the topic to be discussed or information to be gathered or question(s) to be answered. Write this on newsprint and put it up on a wall so everyone can see it.*

C. *Introduce the process by reading the following:*

In order to ensure that everyone who wants to share has the opportunity to speak, we will proceed in the following way:

The leader or a designated person will share first. After that person has spoken, he or she then invites another to share. Whom you invite does not need to be the person next to you. After the next person has

113

spoken, that person is given the privilege to invite another to share. If you don't want to say anything, simply say "pass" and proceed to invite another to share. We will do this until everyone has been invited.

If this is the first time you use this with the group, it will be very awkward at first. The tendency is to give up on the process and go back to the whoever-wants-to-talk-can-talk way. If you are persistent in using this process every time you facilitate the gathering, the group will eventually get used to it and will have great fun with it. A good way to ensure the process goes well the first time is to make sure there are a couple of people in the group who have done this before and, as you begin the process, invite them first.

## Problems to Anticipate:

This process addresses differences in the perception of personal power among the participants. Some people will be eager for their turn, while others will be reluctant to speak when they are invited. If a person speaks very briefly and then does not remember to invite the next person, do not invite for him or her. Simply point out that this person has the privilege to invite the next person to speak. This is especially important if a person "passes." By ensuring that this person still has the privilege to invite, you affirm and value that person independent of that person's verbal ability.

# Appendix B

## *Using Photolanguage in Small Group Communication*

**Objectives:**   (1) To help members of a small group to communicate in a holistic way that engages the visual, the affective, and the intellect.

(2) To help members of a small group to get to know each other and/or to explore a specific topic together.

**Type of Group:**   Any.

**Size of Group:**   8–20.

**Setting:**   A bright, large room. Chairs for participants should be arranged in a circle in one area of the room. In a separate area of the room, set up three or four large tables that can accommodate the display of all the photos without crowding. Make sure there is room around each table for participants to move around. If tables are not available, sometimes displaying the photos on the floor may be acceptable if you have a very bright room.

**Materials:**   A set of Photolanguage: *Interactions*[1] by Eric Law.
Newsprint and markers.

**Time Required:**   One hour or longer depending on the size of the group.

[1]*Interactions* is published by Inspiral Productions. You can purchase a copy by writing: Inspiral Productions, 3175 S. Hoover Street, Box 357, Los Angeles, CA 90007–3164.

*How to Proceed:*

## 1. Preparation

Write the questions you want the participants to explore on the newsprint—large enough to be seen at a distance. Give participants at least two questions: one general and the other more specific. Here are some examples:

*Example A:*
Say "Who are you?"
and/or
"How are you feeling now?"
in one or two photos

*Example B:*
Say "What is racism?"
and/or
"How has racism affected your life?"
and/or
"What is it like being a victim of racism?"
in one, two, or three photos.

*Example C:*
Say "Who are you?"
and/or
"What is your relationship with God?"
in one or two photos.

Example A is a set of questions that helps a group to get to know each other. Example B is a set of questions that helps a group to explore a specific subject. Example C is a set of questions that does both. (*Interaction* by Eric Law is best used to explore relational questions.)

## 2. Instructions to participants

*a. Invite participants to sit in the circle.*

*b. Give the following instructions:*

Very often in group communication, we are asked to express ourselves in words alone. In culturally diverse groups, verbal communication alone is not sufficient because different cultures have varying degrees of comfort with verbal communication. In order to help us communicate better, I have brought a tool with me.

There are about fifty photographs on the tables. Instead of asking you to begin our sharing with words, I invite you to communicate in a different way—that is, with images. There are two (or three) questions posted on the wall. I invite you to answer one or both (or three) questions with one or two (or three) photographs. (*Repeat the questions.*) You can answer one question with two photos or two (or three) questions with one photo or any combination in between. Do not think about what image you want to answer the questions. Rather, just gently plant the questions in your mind and when you are ready, go look at the photographs. Let the photos speak to you first. If a particular photograph catches your attention, stay there and dialogue with the photograph. Ask: Why is this picture catching my attention? Does it answer the questions posted? How?

When you finish the dialogue with the photo, move on. If another picture catches your attention, stay there and do the same thing. Do this until you have looked at all the photographs. When you have done so, mentally pick the photos that you want. Do not pick them up physically because if you do, someone else might miss the chance of sharing those pictures with you. When you have picked your photos mentally, just come back to the circle and sit down. And when everyone comes back to the circle, that means all of you have picked your photos. Is there any question on how we will proceed?

Now, I invite you to be silent for a minute and plant these questions in your mind. (*Repeat the questions again.*) When you are ready, you may go and look at the photos. Please do this in silence.

c. *When everyone comes back, give the following instructions:*

Let's go to pick up our photos. If your photo is not there, that means someone will share that photo with you. Just come back to the circle and see if it is in the circle.

d. *When participants return with their photos, invite them to put the photos facing up on the floor so that everyone can see them. Introduce Mutual Invitation (See Appendix A) as a process for the group to share their photos.*

e. *After everyone has shared, use the rest of the time to draw some connections, syntheses, new insights, common themes, and/or opposites that have come out of the sharing. Stop any psychologizing on a particular person in the group. Limit questions to clarification ones only.*

f. *Closing: There are a variety of ways to end the session depending on the intensity of the sharing. Here are three examples:*

- A group hug.

- Put all the picked photos in the middle of the circle. Invite participants to spend a period of silence to look at the photos and connect the photos with the persons who picked them. Prayers may be offered in silence. End with the Lord's Prayer.

- If the group will use the same room for a longer period of time as in a retreat, put the picked photos on the wall. This can create ownership of the space for the group.

- If this exercise is used in the context of a Eucharist, the picked photos can be placed around the altar during the offertory.

## Problems to Anticipate:

Remember: this is a communication tool, and not a psychological tool. The facilitator must help the participants stay at the communication level and respect what is shared as information offered by the participants. The sharing should not be used to make psychological inferences. One good way to avoid this is to invite people to use "I" statements when making a comment and to ask only clarification questions.

## Origin of the Process:

I learned how to use Photolanguage from Alain Baptiste, one of the originators of this tool, in Lyons, France, in 1980. I have added Mutual Invitation to the process to enhance the use of the tool especially for multicultural groups.

## Other Ways of Using Photolanguage:

I have described a well-tried way of using Photolanguage. There are other ways to use it. Here are some examples:

1. Pick a photo and write a poem from it.

2. Start a story and ask people to continue the story by connecting different photos that they pick. This is good for children.

3. Create a problem from a photo and ask the group to help solve it.

4. Pick a favorite photo. Explain why it is a favorite. Pick the least favorite. Explain why it is not a favorite.

5. Write a dialogue in "balloon" form—as in a comic strip—for the situation in the photo.

# Appendix C

# Community Bible Study

## Preparation:

A leader prepares to lead a Community Bible Study by first looking up the upcoming passage in the lectionary. The leader may choose any one of the three lessons. When a passage is chosen, read it a few times. Write down any questions and words that you don't understand in the passage. Look up the passage in the commentaries[1] and try the best you can to answer the questions of the Research Preparation Form. You should not spend more than forty-five minutes for the research. The goal is not to do a thorough research of the passage, but to get some input from biblical scholarship that will enrich the group's reflection on the passage. Based on your reading, prepare a three- to five-minute report. Present only the context from which the text is taken, the historical information about the book, and the literary style of the text. Leave the interpretation to the participants. It is very important for the leader to stay within the three- to five-minute time limit. The leader should not give the impression that he or she is an expert. (See p. 130f. for the Research Preparation Form.)

Look at the list of questions suggested in Section 4, Step 3. Determine which question you will use for the second-reading reflection. You may want to use a different but more suitable question based on your research. Write the question on newsprint.

---

[1]A good one-volume commentary is the *Jerome Bible Commentary* or the *One-Volume Interpreter's Bible Commentary*. Either will give the leader most of the basic information needed about the particular passage. If more information is needed on a particular theme, word, idea, or place, a good source is *The Interpreter's Dictionary of the Bible*.

## *How to Proceed:*
## *I. Opening Meditation and Prayer*

*The leader invites participants to close their eyes and be silent for one minute. Then, the following meditation is read:*

Take a few deep breaths and exhale slowly. (*Silence*) As you exhale, let go of the tensions and anxieties that you have brought with you so that you can be here fully in this time and space (*Pause*) to be with one another and with God. (*Silence*) Are you willing to let something new happen? (*Silence*) Can you be open to the Spirit of God as it speaks to you through the Bible passage, one another, and in your own hearts? (*Silence*)

*Then the leader reads the following prayer or some other appropriate prayer.*

Let us pray:

O God, who has taught us that your Word is a lantern to our feet and a light to our path: Grant that as this community devoutly reads the Holy Scriptures, we may realize our fellowship one with another in you, and may learn thereby to know you more fully, to love you more truly, and to follow more faithfully in the steps of your Son Jesus Christ; who lives and reigns with you and the Holy Spirit, one God blessed for evermore. Amen.

*The leader reads the following before proceeding:*

Before we start, there is an overall ground rule that needs to be stated: If at anytime during this Bible study, you are asked to do something that you don't want to do, simply say "pass." We do not want to make anybody feel uncomfortable and no one needs to feel pressured.

## *II. Introduction and Purpose*

*1. The following preamble is read:*

The _____(*fill in the name of your organization*) Community Bible Study Group is a fellowship of people who come together to read Scripture and to share our insights, experiences, hopes, and prayers as the Bible passages inspire us. We believe, by doing so, we can become a stronger community of people who pray together, help each other with our problems, and reach out to serve others.

*(If there is no newcomer, the following two paragraphs may be skipped.)*

We believe that the Bible consists of books written by people, under the inspiration of the Holy Spirit, to show God at work in nature and history, to set forth the life and teachings of Jesus, and to proclaim the Good News for all people. We must not deny that the writers, inspired by God, wrote these books in the context of their times and culture, sometimes addressing specific communities. Therefore, we invite the participants to explore the meaning of the text in its historical context as well as its application to our lives today.

The selection of the text to be studied is one of the passages appointed for the following Sunday according to the common lectionary of the Roman Catholic, Episcopal, Lutheran, Methodist, and Presbyterian Churches. We do this because this will better prepare the participants to hear the Word of God on the coming Sunday and this will stop us from reading only those passages that we are comfortable or familiar with. Moreover, the lectionary is a great symbol of Christian unity today.

*2. Invite participants to briefly introduce themselves.*

## IIIA. Ground Rules (Longer Form)[2]

*(The shorter version of the ground rules, immediately following, may be read if there is no newcomer.)*

*The leader gives the following explanation of having ground rules:*

> In order for a group of people to communicate effectively, it must have a common set of ground rules that everyone in the group agrees to keep. The following are some ground rules that we believe to be very important to keep when we come together to read Scripture:

1. The Bible passage, and not the leader or the group, is the focus of this Bible Study.

2. There is no such thing as "the right" interpretation to each text. The wondrous thing about the Bible is that it has room for many different interpretations. Christians for thousands of years have been interpreting and reinterpreting the same passages and probably will be for thousands of years to follow. We are not here to debate who has the right answer, but we are here to read Scripture together and share our insights. The fact is that no one has the whole truth. Only by sharing our insights and various interpretations can we discover the more "complete" shared truth.

3. Our leaders are not experts. They will not "approve" or "disapprove" of what is shared. They are but facilitators who will lead us through a process by which the inspiration from Scriptures can be shared and celebrated. However, a leader might bring in historical and contextual information concerning the text that will provide the essential background for the group to understand the text better.

---

[2]Ground rules one through five are adapted from Walter Wink's *Transforming Bible Study*.

4. Some of us will have extensive background in biblical study. Others will have next to none. Nevertheless, we are all equals before the text, for in regard to our own experiences we are all experts. And since it is the intersection of text with experience that evokes insights, no one needs to feel disadvantaged. In fact, we would invite you to adopt a "beginner's mind," so that every time we approach a text, we would hear it as if for the first time.

5. Because we seek insights and not just information, it is essential that everyone join in the discussion. Those who tend to speak a lot in groups will need to watch themselves to be sure they are not using more than their share of the time, and those who tend to be timid and shy about speaking out in groups need to take responsibility for carrying their fair share of the load.

6. We invite you to hold the personal information shared here in confidence because only in this way can we feel free to say what is in our minds and hearts.

## IIIB. Ground Rules (Shorter Version)

1. The Bible passage, and not the leader or the group, is the focus of this Bible Study.

2. We are not here to debate who has the right interpretation, but we are here to read the Scripture together and share our insights.

3. Our leaders are not experts. They are but facilitators who will lead us through a process by which the inspiration from Scriptures can be shared and celebrated. However, a leader might bring in historical, literary, and contextual information to help the group understand the text better.

4. We are all equals before the Scripture; therefore no one needs to feel disadvantaged. We invite you to adopt a "beginner's mind," so that every time we

approach a text, we would hear it as if for the first time.

5. Because we seek insights and not just information, it is essential that everyone join in the discussion.

6. We invite you to hold the personal information shared here in confidence because only in this way can we feel free to say what is in our minds and hearts.

## IV. The Bible Study Procedure

*The leader reads the following explanation of the Bible study procedure:*

During this Bible study, we will listen to the same Bible passage three times. Each participant will be invited to share his or her insight after each reading. In order to ensure that everyone who wants to share has the opportunity to speak, we will use a process of Mutual Invitation. We will proceed in the following way:

The leader or a designated person will share first. After that person has spoken, he or she then invites another to share. Whom you invite next does not need to be the person next to you. After the next person has spoken, that person is given the privilege to invite another to share. If you don't want to say anything, simply say "pass" and proceed to invite another to share. We will do this until everyone has been invited.

## Step 1

*Invite a member of the group to read the text slowly. Identify which translation of the Bible is being read.*

As _____ reads this passage, I invite you to watch for a word, phrase, or image that speaks to you.

*After the reading, there may be a period of silence.*

Using Mutual Invitation, I now invite you to share a word, phrase, or image in this passage that speaks out to you—without discussion.

## Step 2

*If the leader has some contextual, historical, and literary information about the text or definitions of unfamiliar terms, spend no more than three to five minutes to share it. (See Section on Preparation.)*

## Step 3

*Invite another participant to read the passage a second time.*

As _____ reads this passage again, I invite you to reflect on this question: *(The leader may choose one of the following questions or another suitable question.)*

a) What was the writer trying to say to the people of his or her time?

b) Imagine yourself as one of the characters in the story. *(List all the characters.)* How do you feel as this character, as the story is being read?

c) Where does this passage touch your life today?

d) Where does this biblical story intercept with your life story?

e) What does this passage say about _____? *(Fill in the blank—a theme or subject from the passage.)*

f) Draw a picture that represents _____ in the passage. *(Fill in the blank—a theme or subject from the passage.)*

Time is set aside for reflection (two to three minutes). I now invite you to share your reflection on the question *(repeat question again)* using Mutual Invitation.

## Step 4

*Invite another participant to read the passage again.*

As _____ reads the passage the third time, I invite you to reflect on the questions: How does God invite you to change? What does God invite you to do through this passage?

*The text is read. Time is set aside for reflection.*

Now I invite you to share your insights on how God invites you to change and what God invites you to do through this passage using Mutual Invitation again.

*Take a ten-minute break.*

## V. Community Sharing

*Invite the participants to gather together again. Then read the following:*

The next half hour is set aside for us to share with each other our concerns and requests for prayers that are inspired by our faith and the study of the Holy Scriptures. (*"Concerns" can be replaced by planning, hopes, dreams, visions, struggles, problems, good news, ministries, etc. depending on the spirit of the group.*) In order to ensure that everyone has a chance to share, we will continue to use the Mutual Invitation process. If you don't have anything to share, just say, "pass." After that, we will open up the floor for anyone who wishes to share more.

*At the end of the sharing time, the leader uses one of the following ways to close the session:*

*1. Invite the group to complete the following sentences on a piece of paper:*

"I thank God today _____."

"I ask God today _____."

*Close the session by inviting each participant to read these sentences as prayers. Conclude the session with the Lord's Prayer.*

*2. Have a period of silence and invite participants to offer their prayers and petitions. Conclude with the Lord's Prayer.*

3. *Invite each participant to ask the person on his or her right to keep her in his prayers in the coming week. This could be very specific or general. When everyone has done that, keep a period of silence and conclude with the Lord's Prayer.*

## VI. Closing Remarks

*The following is read to welcome new leaders of future sessions:*

The leadership of this Community Bible Study group is shared. Anyone in the group who wishes to lead a session is encouraged to talk to the coordinator of the group and he or she will help you with the resources you need in order to prepare for it.

If this Bible study proves to be meaningful to you, we invite you to share this with another by inviting your friends to come in the future.

*Then, the following is read:*

In closing, I would like to thank all of you for sharing. From the things you've heard in this last hour, take what you like and leave the rest. Talk with each other; pray for each other; but let there be no gossip, judgment, or criticism of one another. Instead, let the Word, understanding, love, and peace of God and of this fellowship grow in you day after day in your lives and work until we meet again.

## COMMUNITY BIBLE STUDY
## RESEARCH PREPARATION FORM

BIBLE PASSAGE: _____

BIBLICAL CONTEXT:

What is the book as a whole about? How does this text relate to the whole?

What goes before this text? What goes after this text?

What is the function of the passage in its context? (I.e., is it a climax, conclusion, summary, turning point, supporting argument, etc.?)

FORM:

What is the literary form/genre of the text? Is it a parable, sermon, narrative, saying, song, poem, used in worship, letter, etc.?

What does the literary form tell about the text's meaning and purpose?

Would you read the passage differently the second time in order to help the participants to understand the text better?

WORD STUDY:

What are the key terms in this text?

What other words are not readily understandable by the participants?

What meaning do they have in this context?

## TRANSLATION:

Compare several translations; how do these inform the task of interpretation?

Is there anything that the participants need to know in order to capture the essence of its original Hebrew or Greek text?

## HISTORICAL CONTEXT:

What are the cultural, political, socioeconomic, and theological contexts of the author? Of the audience?

Is there a question as to "what really happened"?

These questions may not apply to all the passages. Therefore, you may not have answers to all the questions. Review your answers again and write out a three-to-five-minute report.